A
Feminist
Tarot

A *Sally Gearhart*
Susan Rennie

Feminist
Tarot

Boston · Alyson Publications, Inc.

This is a trade paperback from Alyson Publications, Inc.,
40 Plympton Street, Boston, Mass. 02118.
Distributed in England by GMP Publishers,
P.O. Box 247, London N17 9QR, England.
Available in braille from Humboldt Braille Transcribers,
P.O. Box 6363, Eureka, California 95501.

Published by Persephone Press, 1976.

Fifth edition

5   4   3

ISBN 0-932870-56-2

Preface

Since the last printing of *A Feminist Tarot* we have been heartened by the increase in interest in the Tarot in general and by the enthusiastic response to this book in particular. That response has come from men as well as from women, from those "apolitically identified" as well as from feminists. Some women's critical remarks have been helpful in our revision of the book for this new edition. Particularly we would like to acknowledge Jane Gurko, without whose critical faculties the revision would never have been accomplished. We are grateful, too, for the help given us by Gloria Anzaldua, Kirsten Grimstad, Christine Menefee, Louisiana Sissies in Struggle, Alyse B. Tartell, and Joyce and other Sisters of Aradia.

The text of the book has been somewhat altered to include our own changing perspectives and our responses to constructive criticism. We hope that the new introduction and bibliography will increase the book's usefulness. We still see *A Feminist Tarot* as only a beginning in women's recovery of the Tarot from traditional masculinist bias. And we still acknowledge that the views expressed here have their own limitations. Our hope is that the work we have done will aid others in uncovering more of the meanings inherent in the cards so that the Tarot becomes truly an instrument for women's self-discovery and self-exploration.

Since the last printing of this book its original publisher, Persephone Press, has been forced to cease operations. Both of us, Susan and Sally, want to express again our gratitude to the women of Persephone not only for their commitment to women's culture but as well for the fairness, straightforwardness, and willingness to struggle which characterized our association with them. Persephone Press, from its inception in 1976, gave the women's movement access to an astonishing amount of lesbian feminist and feminist literature; some of their publications have become classics. So even while we mourn the loss of Persephone, we cherish its gifts and acknowledge its vision of lesbian publishing. The women's movement and the lesbian/gay movement share a fundamental need of publishing houses that can risk the publication of books that represent us. One such publishing house has been *A Feminist Tarot*'s present publisher, Alyson Publications. Its owner, Sasha Alyson, took over a number of Persephone's titles and has seen to it that they remain available to the movement and to the world at large. Our association with Sasha and the staff of Alyson Publications has been from the outset a pleasure and a benefit. We're glad to be a part of that enterprise and its commitment to the spread of lesbian, feminist, and gay literature.

Sally M. Gearhart
San Francisco

Susan Rennie
Los Angeles

Contents

Introduction

After the publication of *A Feminist Tarot* in 1976 women frequently questioned us about our use of a traditional deck. Why hadn't we used a new, feminist-envisioned Tarot to accompany our feminist interpretations? The current renaissance of interest in the Tarot has resulted in at least a dozen newly-conceived decks whose images are considerably changed from the traditional images of the Tarot trumps and the minor arcana, familiar to us since Waite published his deck in 1911. These have included at least one "woman's" deck in which the images have been drastically altered to eliminate what the author sees as patriarchal and masculinist bias. We applaud these new developments, particularly as they contribute to our women's culture, and we hope for their continued success.

But a large part of the answer to the original question—our choice of the Waite-Smith deck—has to do with our understanding of what the Tarot is, our beliefs about its historical lineage, our conception of its use and function. We feel that the power of the Tarot derives from an ancient and complex symbology that represents all aspects, forces, stages, configurations in our psychic lives—a totality of human experience. The traditional Tarot, with all its richness and mystery, can be a woman's Tarot. That, essentially, is what we have attempted to show: the re-appropriation of meaning within the original matrix. The "old" cards, seen from an altered angle of vision, can be used as a tool for self-analysis—to explore our inner regions, to give ear to our inner voices; they still activate the potent insights and connections which it has been the purpose of the Tarot to evoke. In fact, if we look at its ancestry we will see that the Tarot is a particularly appropriate vehicle for women with feminist consciousness. At its very core it is synchronous with that vision which honors the female principle as a creative and dynamic force in the universe.

There are a number of fanciful myths about the origins of the Tarot. One of the most popular stories is that it was introduced into western Europe by the Gypsies; another, that it was produced at a gathering of sages and wise men at Fez. The Gypsy theory speculates that these itinerant people made their way into Europe over the course of several centuries, carrying with them the wisdom of ancient Egypt whence they came —hence "Gypsy." The wisdom was encoded in the Tarot, which they used in a debased form as a method of fortune-telling. There is even a "Tarot" deck, the Grand Etteila of the Gypsies, which is based on this myth, but which resembles traditional decks in little else than name. The wise men story explains the Tarot as a book of symbols representing the synthesized esoteric knowledge of the ancient, pre-Christian world put together at a convention of sages and adepts sometime after the burning of the great library at Alexandria. Their purpose was to keep that knowledge alive in the face of an advancing, militant, monolithic Christian patriarchy.

These stories may contain a kernel of truth, as we shall see, but there is simply no evidence to substantiate their claims. The Gypsies, in fact, came not from Egypt but from India and they reached western Europe about 100 years after the Tarot had appeared in France and Italy. The only factual evidence we have about the origins of the Tarot are seventeen exquisitely painted cards now in the Bibliotheque Nationale in Paris. We know that these cards can be dated to 1392 because of an entry in a ledger by a court treasurer to Charles VI of France noting that a particular amount of money had been paid to the artist Jacquemin Gringoneur for three packs of these cards. This is the first documented appearance of the Tarot. About thirty years after Gringoneur was paid for his deck Bonifacio Bembo painted a deck for the Duke of Milan. This Visconti deck (taking the family name of the reigning house of Milan) is the first full Tarot deck of which we have any record. Prior to these dates there is nothing—no cards, no literary or historical reference *anywhere*. Whether or not Gringoneur and Bembo were the authors of the decks they painted, whether they copied existing decks or were instructed in what to paint, we do not know. It is true that the Marseilles deck, first published in the seventeenth century, is considered by many scholars on internal evidence such as costuming and decorative motifs to date to the early fourteenth century, that is, before Gringoneur's cards. And it is likely that the lavish cards painted for the French Court were copied from some existing deck—which, if it were so, would take the earliest Tarot to the early 1300s. Any information we have to indicate an earlier existence is hypothetical. There are only clues, suggestions, from which all sorts of theories have been constructed.

All speculations agree in one particular: that the Tarot is a *book* of knowledge, "an encyclopedia of magical memory images," as Paul Huson has called it, representing a system of mystical wisdom encoded in the pictures of the twenty-two trumps and in the numerology of the fifty-six minor suit cards. Hypotheses are generally more persuasive when they are not inconsistent with known evidence, when, in fact they are congruent with the given facts. If we look at the period in which the Tarot first appeared—or first surfaced—there is much to support this notion of its being a pictorially camouflaged belief system.

The late fourteenth and early fifteenth centuries was a period during which the Church was truly becoming the Church Militant—flexing its muscles in the battle to suppress all non-Christian and non-patriarchal expressions of religion. In particular it attempted to suppress the Old Religion, the gnostic heresies flourishing in northern Italy and southern France (the Waldenses, Cathari, Albigenses), the Jews, and social dissenters such as homosexuals. The Church went after these deviant groups with zeal and determination. Most were systematically, literally, burned out of Christian Europe. The extirpation of the major Cathar heresy in the Languedoc—a region of southern France where in large areas it was the dominant religion—was carried out through a series of crusades mounted by the French monarchy (wielding the sword for the Church) with such a degree of thoroughness that there is today no evidence of this large, well-organized, sophisticated sect except the Church's own records of their persecution and destruction. Similarly we have no evidence except what has survived in Church documents of the beliefs, rituals, and practices of the Old Religion.

It makes sense that faced with this kind of onslaught the keepers of non-Christian, esoteric, and perhaps orally-based doctrine would look for some way to secure its preservation and survival—intact from the Church. What better way than in picture cards, used in a gambling game (tarocchi was the Italian game for which the Visconti deck was designed), or used for that other timeless passion which people everywhere seem to share—fortune-telling? And what better way than to have the picture cards represent familiar cultural figures (the Fool, the Pope, the Emperor, the Hermit) and homilies (Temperance, Justice, Judgement)? And jokes—because the idea of a female pope was certainly a joke on the Church. True, one card fails to fit so easily into medieval popular culture—the mysterious and provocative Hanged Man. But even this card could be passed off as a criminal on the gallows, a familiar enough part of medieval scenery (although how often appearing upside down is another matter).

Using pictures as a storage device, a highly elaborate filing/retrieval system, was a well-developed medieval technique. In fact, commentators occasionally point to the medieval *ars memorativa* or mnemonics by which pictorial images arranged in a special order could be used to release whole categories of mental associations; they see mnemonics as the ideal vehicle for encoding an elaborate and complex cosmological/metaphysical oral tradition. Pictorial encoding was not only safer; in an age when writing was a restricted art it made messages more accessible. Of course Christian vigilantes eventually tumbled to what they suspected were the inherent dangers of these innocent-looking game cards. As early as the 1420s preachers were inveighing against card gaming and fortune telling as an invention of Satan, and to this day the Tarot is known in some parts of Europe as "the Devil's picturebook." But luckily, by this time, the cards were too widespread to be suppressed.

If one strips away the names—Pope, Papess, Emperor, Hermit, Juggler —what is left are powerful images which are anything but Christian in origin, anything but patriarchal in inference, and certainly of much greater antiquity than the superficial medieval stereotypes would suggest. It is true that the cards show the influence of the medieval culture in which they were presumably first translated from oral wisdom to painted pictures; but we should remember that even so it is through the mesh of dissident and defiant medieval Europe that they were filtered.

The images of the Tarot, their symbolism, can be traced back to the gnostic cults that thrived in the early Christian era, cults which in turn blended elements of Greek philosophy and Jewish mysticism with Indian and Persian metaphysical teachings, Egyptian mystery rites, with some seasoning of Christian doctrine. Most occult historians locate the occult arts of the West—including alchemy and astrology, in addition to the Tarot—in this early melange of gnosticism. "Gnostic" itself is a Greek derivation for "someone who knows," a wise man or woman; "wicce," the Anglo-Saxon derivation of witch, means the craft of the wise woman or man. In both instances the strong implication is that the wisdom is part of an esoteric or hidden tradition.

We know, even if from unfriendly sources, that dissident cults were activated again in the twelfth and thirteenth centuries in the heretical sects of the regions in Europe where the Tarot made its first known appearance. We also know that at this time Jews, particularly Spanish Jews, were moving to the more hospitable climate of the Languedoc because of mounting Church persecution. So hospitable to the Jews were the Cathar dissidents that one of the principal indictments of their heresy, formally listed by the Church Inquisition, was that Cathar communities extended full citizenship to Jews and allowed their participation in civic affairs.

It is documented by a wrathful Church that in times of trouble Cathars hid Jews and Jews hid Cathars, depending on who was taking the heat. More interestingly, certain Jewish mystics, who were looked at askance by their own orthodox community, found refuge among the Cathars, whose effulgent and efflorescing culture represented an openness and receptivity to new ideas extraordinary in the history of Europe. This welcome Jewish presence among the French heretics could provide one of the keys to the origin of the Tarot—again an entirely speculative connection, but enormously suggestive, as we shall see.

So far as we know, the Tarot languished until the eighteenth century, being used only as a fortune-telling tool by the Gypsies of Spain and southern France as well as by the *strege* or wise women of Italy. In the eighteenth century coincident with a resurgence of interest in the occult, the Tarot was "rediscovered" by scholars, Masons, and Rosicrucians who realized that the cards amounted to much more than fortune-telling devices. In the nineteenth century Eliphas Levi, a French Rosicrucian and occult scholar, uncovered the provocative correspondences between the Tarot and the Kabbalah. This relationship is an important clue in understanding the Tarot as a very rich and meaningful system of cosmology. Indeed, it is a connection which identifies the Tarot as the repository of ancient wisdom hinted at in the myths of its origin: a symbolic system of objective knowledge which provides answers to some of our oldest, perennial questions about the nature of the universe. For the Kabbalah is an underground body of Jewish mystical knowledge which is quite basic to all western occultism. It is nothing less than the original (and suppressed) cosmology of which the first four books of the Old Testament are a distortion, a distortion which enthroned patriarchy at the expense of a more female-oriented belief system.

The Hebrew alphabet contains twenty-two letters, the same number, of course, as the Tarot trumps. Kabbalists attribute special spiritual power and significance to each letter—in fact, arranged on the connecting paths of a glyph known as the Tree of Life, they provide an understanding of the cosmos. Thus, positing a correspondence between these letters and the twenty-two major arcana gives the cards an immediate kabbalistic interpretation. The Kabbalah is also concerned with the four letters of

God's name, YHVH, which represent, among other things, the four worlds of creation, the four stages of existence, and the four basic elements: fire, water, air, earth. There are four court cards in each of the four Tarot suits. And each suit is identified with one of the four elements: pentacles/earth, wands/fire, swords/air, cups/water. Then the Kabbalah works with the number ten—the ten sephiroth or emanations (connected by the twenty-two paths). The four Tarot suits consist of cards numbered one through ten. Further, the *Zohar*—a collection of Kabbalistic wisdom which states among other things that male and female exist in all created things—was first published in the fourteenth century, roughly the same time that the Tarot appeared. Even though it is true that in the published writings of the Kabbalah there is no mention of the Tarot, still the correlations and connections seem to go on and on.

The ways in which the Tarot can be used as a meditational and mystical system in conjunction with the Kabbalistic Tree of Life are far too complex to go into here. However, we do hope to expand the next edition of *A Feminist Tarot* to include an exploration of the Tree of Life from a feminist perspective because, like so much else, the Kabbalah has presumably suffered alterations, distortions, accretions in its passage through masculinist culture. What is important for us here is that the Kabbalah is a system of wisdom about the universe and our place in it which acknowledges the dynamic force of the female principle. It correlates with the other non-patriarchal beliefs which also appear to have contributed to the symbolism of the Tarot.

We speculate that the Tarot was the product of a synthesis—a synergistic association—between on the one hand the bearers of an ancient, pre-patriarchal tradition and, on the other, the practitioners of an "heretical" belief-system which resonated with the ancient beliefs and which were anathema to the Christian Church. Both the ancient and the "heretical" strands were sharply different from the anti-nature, anti-woman dogmatism of the Christian-centered warp of western culture. In true gnostic tradition, for example, Cathar women served equally with men in what were sacerdotal roles—one of their most horrendous heresies. We also know that Cathars in the ministry were vegetarians, sworn to observe the sanctity of all living creatures. We don't know what their esoteric beliefs were, but the Church considered them worthy of a hundred years' holy war; and if the Cathars were consistent with what we know of other strands of gnosticism, they were not patriarchal. Future scholarship will probably unveil other striking consistencies between ancient pre-patriarchal traditions and the non-patriarchal practices of medieval heretics.

What is also important about the putative link between the Kabbalah and the Tarot is the very clear suggestion that the images are not random, parochial symbols, but an ordered system of ancient archetypes. First and foremost this is the essence of the cards: they are archetypes of the unconscious, seed ideas which evoke specific intellectual and emotional responses. Their principal function is to trigger hidden springs of knowledge allowing us to make conscious connections. The way in which these particular images enliven or potentiate our imagination, yielding mysterious benefits in divination far greater than should be expected, has been well known to occultists of the past as well as to those of the present. To discard the images, or to change them beyond recognition, would risk losing their particular power, that of bringing into consciousness the connections which are so revealing and enlightening.

Our speculations bring us to the question of divination. Why use the Tarot? And why use the Waite-Smith deck? As we wrote in the Introduction to the previous edition of *A Feminist Tarot*, "The querent (the one asking the question) and/or the reader (if the reader differs from the querent) could as easily read about the question from a marbletop table, tea leaves or raindrops on a windowpane—from any configuration or set of symbols conducive to focusing on the vibrations surrounding the question." Theoretically, focusing attention on what would otherwise be a random distribution of variables stimulates the unconscious in some unknown way, and in some equally unknown way the position of the variables being considered is presumably affected. Any system will yield some sort of information; the value of that information, though, depends on the intrinsic wisdom of that system. Each Tarot picture is by itself a rich and deeply evocative set of symbols which relates to the core experiences of the human condition and the human psyche; in the patterns that the Tarot cards form in any chosen spread—with whatever meanings assigned to the various positions—they can yield rich and complex insights in understanding ourselves, because unlike tea leaves or raindrops they were *designed* to yield these patterns. That's why we think it is vital to use a deck that maintains the essential integrity of the original images as does, for example, the Waite-Smith deck.

There are numerous Tarot decks, both historical and contemporary, which exhibit striking differences in style and form but which maintain the basic integrity of the images. There are, for example, widely differing representations of Death, but the *concept* of Death is there unmistakably. In more recent times, many of the decks that have been redesigned elaborate the cards' symbolism—reflecting the extensive information about the Tarot excavated by nineteenth century occult scholars. The changes are an attempt not so much to express the personal world view of the authors (as do decks such as the New Tarot, the Witches' Tarot, the Aquarian Tarot), as to "get it right." The three best known contemporary decks—the Waite-Smith, Paul Foster Case's BOTA, and Crowley's Thoth—are all examples of the attempt to construct a Tarot which is the "true," the "rectified," or the "restored" deck (words used by both Waite and Crowley). (Incidentally, all three of these decks were painted by women: Pamela Coleman-Smith, Jessie Burns Parke, and Frieda Harris, respectively. How much the artists contributed to the conceptualization we don't know.) The significance of these three decks (as well as the recently published but aesthetically disappointing Regardie-Wang deck) is the membership of Waite, Case, and Crowley in the secret Hermetic Order of the Golden Dawn. This was an occult society founded in England in 1888 dedicated to the continuation of ancient esoteric tradition through the study and practice of the Western occult arts. For our purposes, it is very important to note that women were not only admitted and participated in the society on an equal basis with men, but that the beliefs and rituals of the Golden Dawn were Goddess-centered.

The Golden Dawn lasted a scant fifteen years, but its influence, especially on the Tarot, has been enormous. Virtually every major Tarot deck of the twentieth century is derived from the deck used by the members of the Order. That deck, in turn, was the product of deep research and study by one of its founders, MacGregor Mathers, and—a fact rarely mentioned in works on the history of the Tarot—his wife Moina, who frequently conducted the Order's ceremonies in the role of High Priestess. The deck incorporates a virtual archeology of the symbolism of the Tarot including the numerological and astrological significances of the cards, their Kabbalistic correspondences, the importance of colors, and even such details as the relevance of which way figures in the cards faced. The Golden Dawn claimed to be the inheritor of ancient keys to psychic power handed down through the centuries by means of a hidden oral tradition. It was not only the intensive research which had gone into the history of the Tarot that gave the Golden Dawn deck its special puissance, members claimed, but their access to this secret oral tradition

The society's research and its claim to special information may explain the particularly compelling quality of the decks published by its members, most specifically the Waite-Smith, the Case and the Crowley decks. While we cannot say that there is any such thing as a "true" deck, of the three the Waite-Smith deck seems the most symbolically powerful and useful to us. It is more widely available and better known than Case's BOTA, even though there is little difference in detail between the two. Crowley's Thoth deck, for all its seductive and stunning beauty, rouses in us strong reservations of conscience since it was designed by a man who exhibited a vicious and infamous hatred of women.

However, all existing decks pose very real problems for feminists, Waite-Smith's included. Many women do not find offense in the traditional imagery of the Tarot. What has been a sore spot has been the rampant masculinist bias in the traditional interpretations, the meanings attributed to the cards—even by sensitive women Tarotists such as Eden Gray. This was the original impulse behind A Feminist Tarot: to develop meanings which the cards evoke in a feminist imagination.

But interpretation is not the only problem. Some women have found offense in what they see as visual sex-role stereotyping in the pictures themselves. We have hoped that A Feminist Tarot would challenge this depiction of women in the cards

The matter of other caste-marked (meaning those who cannot hide) groups is different. Pictorially all the decks we know of ignore the physically disabled and people of color. There are some tired people in the cards, some blindfolded and even wounded; but there is only one pair of crutches evident (the five of pentacles), and the parade of fully perceptive, physically active, able-bodied characters is overwhelming. It is true that blindness, deafness and much physical disability are not always apparent and should not be hauled out for caste-marking even by well-intentioned artists or interpreters. But the question of disability must permeate our awareness and influence our interpretations wherever possible.

The matter of race in the cards is more obvious. No amount of argument about the origin of the Tarot among dark-skinned people, no cataloging the changes the cards have been subjected to by white European cultures, and no rhapsodizing about the universality of the concepts represented can minimize the effect of the blond and fair-skinned personae who dominate the cards' imagery. We consider this a particularly limiting characteristic of the Waite-Smith deck. It is true that the Tarot, like other artifacts, rises out of a specific culture; and perhaps we should be able to transpose into global terms the specifics of that culture—costumes, properties, settings, and the white skins. But one reason why people of color may not use the Tarot, particularly decks full of human forms, is precisely because such transformations are not worth the hassle. It is true that the Crowley deck with its overall bizarre colors and its nonhuman symbols in the majority of suit cards may allow for more universal interpretation; it is also true that Case's BOTA deck comes without color so that the user can paint the drawings—including skin patches—for most meaningful interpretation. But even such suggestions seem like sops and do not adequately address the problem of the predominantly Caucasian figures suggested in all the decks. We have decided after careful consideration of this issue that the most important factor in dealing with the problem in all the traditional decks and in the Waite-Smith deck in particular may simply be our open acknowledgement of the limitations and our openness to the experience and viewpoint of people of color in the interpretations of the cards themselves. Even in spite of these limitations, the Waite-Smith deck still harbors for us a greater richness and power in its images than other decks. We want to continue its exploration with full acknowledgment of these questions.

Finally, the matter of caste-marked figures and the need for wide boundaries in interpretation bring up an equally significant political matter. How can we use the study of the occult (the I Ching, the Tarot, astrology, the Kabbalah) to encourage dialogue between the "hard core politicos" who supposedly scorn such approaches and the so-called "spiritual" feminists who are accused of retreatism and political irresponsibility?

We both feel that such divisions are more often manufactured among us than inherent in feminist politics, even though we also acknowledge that human beings differ in their approaches to reality. We both think of ourselves as political activists *and* as spiritually concerned feminists. We believe that a consideration of both the "material" and the "psychic" is necessary to the growth of individuals and to the development of feminism as a global force. We hope that "hard core politicos" will remain open to the messages that can come from meditation or from sources beyond hectic daily experience; we hope that feminists who learn and grow from the occult do not let their politics end there but see the necessity for carrying that creative energy into concrete social action. It seems to us that by affirming each other and our differing approaches to reality we can only gain in mutual support and political power.

Using the Tarot

Reading the Cards

Reading the Tarot is an attempt to perceive and understand the conscious and unconscious reality surrounding a particular question or circumstance. What is important in a Tarot reading is whatever is discovered. The discovery is limited only by the reader's openness and sensitivity to the meaning of the cards. Sensitivity grows with acquaintance with the deck and practice in exploring relationships of symbols to particular questions.

The reading should be regarded as a meditation. Before beginning the reader should try to center her energy and quiet down the activity of her conscious mind. This can usually be achieved by doing a few deep breathing and relaxation exercises. While shuffling and cutting the cards the reader should try to keep her mind clear but focused on the cards, while the querent (if she differs from the reader) should concentrate on the question being explored. The reader shuffles the cards and asks the querent to cut them three times to the left with the left hand. The querent then hands the cards back to the reader and the lay-out begins.

Reversed Cards

There are varied opinions on the significance of *reversed* cards. Some readers contend that the dialectic of both positive and negative is inherent in every card, and thus do not read a *reversed card* as any different from an *upright* card. Others read *reversed* cards as an unstable quality to be applied to the upright interpretation. Still others consider the *reversed* card to be very different from the *upright* interpretations. We have used a combination of the latter two approaches; thus readers may ignore the reversed interpretations or take into account our suggestions.

The Court Cards

It seems, judging from our own experience and that of women who have talked with us, that the Court cards present one of the most puzzling and challenging aspects of reading Tarot. Most traditional interpreters see the Court cards as actual men and women connected with the querent and her question. For example, the King of Wands is a "blond, married man of authority; a devoted friend"; the Princess or Page of Cups is a "captivating boy or girl; studious, friendly" (Eden Gray). Others attribute to the Court cards particular personality attributes characteristics such as strength or authority (King of Swords), kindness or generosity (Queen of Wands). There are other formulas; but somehow they have not worked satisfactorily for us.

About a year after *A Feminist Tarot* was published one of us received in the mail some xeroxed pages entitled *The Psychic Tarot* by Joanne

Kowalski. Included was a short discussion of how to read the cards, as well as a discussion of their meanings. We were struck by the clarity and sense of the interpretations—which have provided one of the most helpful sources shaping our own perceptions. But, in particular, we were taken by this woman's approach to the Court cards. This approach has made a difference in our understanding of these cards in a spread, and we want to share this information with our readers. (To our knowledge, *The Psychic Tarot* is not available in book form.) We thank Joanne for her illuminating contributions. Here is what Ms. Kowalski says about the Court cards:

> The king and queen refer to self-security with regard to the attributes represented by their suits and the page (princess) and knight (prince) to the active use of these attributes. Thus, the kings stand for feelings of security regarding the self's ability to perform the activities represented by the suit and the queen, self-security in receiving (learning, getting in touch with, etc.) the attributes of the suit. The knight (prince) is the active doer, the symbolization of actually performing and going out with the qualities of the suit while the page (princess) is the seeker for new horizons, the student, the receiver of ideas and feelings.

Thus, taking Wands as the suit that represents energy and growth, we would suggest that the King of Wands represents the querent's security *in* her own changes and development. The Queen would indicate the querent's security in her own *potentiality* for growth and change, or her security in her ability to accept the growth and change of others. The Knight or Prince would show that the querent is actively involved in change and development, while the Page or Princess would indicate that the querent is seeking growth and change in the matter being considered in the reading. And so with the other suits.

Spreads

The most popular spread in use today is the so-called Celtic spread originally published by Waite in *The Pictorial Key to the Tarot* (1910). This spread is supposed to be the most suitable for obtaining an answer to a definite question.

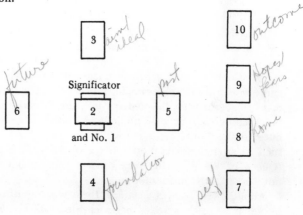

Significator

1. **What Covers Her**—This card gives the influence which is affecting the person or matter of inquiry generally, the atmosphere of it in which the other currents work.

2. **What Crosses Her**—This shows the nature of the obstacles in the matter. If it is a favorable card the opposing forces will not be serious.

3. **What Crowns Her**—This represents the querent's aim or ideal in the matter, or the best that can be achieved under the circumstances.

4. **What is Beneath Her**—This shows the foundation or the basis of the matter, that which has already passed into actuality.

5. **What is Behind Her**—This gives the influence that has passed, or is now passing away.

6. **What is Before Her**—Shows the influence that is coming into action and will operate in the new future.

7. **Herself**—The person's position or attitude toward the question.

8. **Her House**—Her environment and the tendencies at work therein which have an effect on the matter—for instance, the influence of family or immediate friends.

9. **Her Hopes and Fears**—The card shows either what she hopes or fears in the matter.

10. **What Will Come**—The final result, the culmination which is brought about by the other cards that have turned up in the divination.

Dorothy Riddle, a lesbian-feminist astrologer and clinical psychologist from Arizona, suggests the following lay-out as a variation on the traditional Celtic spread:

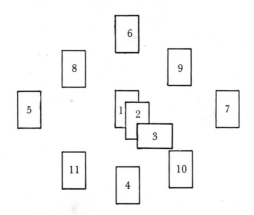

1. Significator

2. Atmosphere or Covering Card—the atmosphere surrounding the question

3. Crossing Card—influences in opposition to the atmosphere, for good or bad; always read upright

4. Foundation—the habits, mindset, value system out of which the question arises

5. Immediate Past—the influence on the question which is presently passing away

6. Possible Future—one of the things that might come to pass

7. Immediate Future—what is likely to happen

8. The Self in Approaching Space—self-concept in regard to the matter

9. Hopes and Fears—what the querent hopes and/or fears about the question

10. Environment—influences and/or attitudes of those near to the querent toward the question

11. The X-Factor—sometimes interpreted as the *outcome*; this spread suggests that this card represents an additional element which the querent may or may not have considered in relation to the matter

There are dozens of other spreads. In the Bibliography we have indicated those books which provide guides to interesting and useful ways of patterning the cards for various kinds of divination.

We have also included the traditional meanings of the cards so that the reader herself may compare the distinctiveness of the feminist interpretations, at the same time noting their kinship with the historical Tarot.

A
Feminist
Tarot

The Major Arcana

0
THE FOOL
(Planet Uranus)

Upright: NAIVETE

An androgynous youth begins a journey, a task, a challenge. She is fresh, innocent, not operating under controlled ego but garbed in insouciance or non-responsibility. She experiences the world without the self-consciousness that often blocks enlightenment. She is unable to prepare for the journey except by the experience itself of starting. She sets out optimistically. Only the dog—consort of the Great Mother—warns of an approaching peril.

An optimistic beginning; ebullience, over-confidence. Innocent trust of people and situations. The Fool, wearing the rags-and-tatters of the troubador, plays to the audience, constantly seeks those who will enjoy her. She is an outsider who is mocked and laughed at, but who is the harbinger of real change.

The querent is approaching an indiscrete beginning; perhaps some thoughtless action, possible folly. A risk is imminent, and an important choice has to be made. She may need to accept the fact that she will make mistakes.

The card can also suggest wanderlust, the call of some place or mission or adventure.

Traditional meaning:

Venturesome quest. Spiritual innocence containing within it cosmic wisdom. The dreamer confronted with choices.

Reversed: RELUCTANCE

Not yet ready to make a beginning; ill-prepared even to risk the experience of learning. The time is not right for some new enterprise or undertaking. Major problems will be created by impulsive behavior.

Perhaps some stubbornness or desire to sustain status quo; inability to take an important risk; fear of the future. Perhaps disillusionment as a result of too many false starts; jaded or cynical.

The querent or one near her may be too self-conscious to act spontaneously. Or she may fear being laughed at, being thought foolish. She may hold back her creativity out of fear of being thought a freak.

Traditional reversed meaning:

Thoughtlessness, carelessness, folly, inconsiderate or unconsidered action.

4

THE MAGICIAN.

1
THE MAGICIAN
(Planet Mercury)

Upright: CHANNELIZATION
(also Creative Will Power)

The Magician is the agent, the wise channel of consciousness. The consciousness flows two ways. The figure does not "draw" power from above, but opens her/himself at both extremes so as to connect two entities, fields, areas, things, people. A mutual movement takes place through the Magician: the dark synthesizing powers of the psyche rush to meet the bright analytical powers of the mental. Light makes materiality aware of itself and the dark gives spirit something to be aware of. Experiences are illuminated; thoughts are embodied; language may be born. The Magician is the channel.

The querent or one near her needs some channel or connection. Or she may serve as some connection. There is much dealing with power here: personal, political or cosmic. Analysis and synthesis; organization; meaning-bestowing.

The querent may be a mediator or may need a mediator.

Also a unifying card. All the major symbols (wands, cups, swords, pentacles) are gathered in one place and the moebius strip or cosmic lemniscate suggests the infinite connectedness of all things.

Traditional meaning:
Strength of will. Originality, creativity.

Reversed: BLOCKED POWER
Some deliberate destructive use of power affecting the querent's life. Or lack of responsibility or maturity in handling power; an inept channel. Perhaps presumptuousness in addressing energy or refusal to share power or energy with others. Some lack of understanding of energy or a giving of precedence to one kind of power over another. Blockage of circuits; lack of connection; isolation from forces of creativity or meaning.

The querent or one near her experiences scattered and short-lived bursts of energy, but no real source of power. There is a lack of connectedness of her powers, no synthesis of reason, sensation, intuition, feeling.

Traditional reversed meaning:
Weakwilled, failure of nerve, indecision. The use of one's powers for destructive purposes.

5

2
THE HIGH PRIESTESS
(Planet Moon)

THE HIGH PRIESTESS

Upright: HIDDEN KNOWLEDGE

The virgin, the one-unto-herself, the daughter of the moon, the unconquered, the lesbian, the witch, Isis, Artemis, Diana, Lilith. She is shrouded in the mystery of the as yet unrevealed. "There are some respects in which this card is the highest and holiest of the greater arcana." (Waite)

The Priestess holds the sacred Torah suggesting the matriarchal roots that underlie patriarchy. She represents men's deepest fear: that women do not need men.

The querent's future is hidden, unknown, virginal. Or some aspects of the querent (or one near her) are virginal. She is in touch with hidden knowledge, perhaps to be expressed creatively. Some important aspects of a situation seem unknowable, but will be revealed if she is open to the worlds of the psyche. Intuitive perception will help solve old problems.

Traditional meaning:

Hidden influences at work. Intuition, perception.

Reversed: FORCED KNOWLEDGE
(also Superficial Knowledge)

Reliance on surface or rational knowledge—with no regard for deeper, more pervasive sources. Acceptance of patriarchal norms about perception and truth.

Information taken by force; the raped mind. Exploitation of the intellectual, bodily or creative/psychic functions. Forcing a situation; bursting in where angels fear to tread; trying to move something prematurely.

Or frustrated knowledge, the sense of some deep message that cannot be made conscious; the on-the-tip-of-my-tongue feeling never satisfied.

The querent or one near is approaching a situation too directly. Or she is in danger of being raped intellectually, physically, psychically. Perhaps she does work that another gets credit for or otherwise sacrifices her intellect.

Traditional reversed meaning:

Surface knowledge. Lack of understanding, foresight. Shallowness.

THE EMPRESS.

3
THE EMPRESS
(Planet Venus)

Upright: FERTILITY

Earth Mother, Venus, the eternal resource, she from whom all come and to whom all return. Love, productivity, generative forces. The holder and carrier of seeds to fruition. Usually the heterosexual woman. But also that aspect of all women in touch with physically, sensually-derived energy.

A time or circumstance for great growth of any kind. Special bountifulness for creative and artistic people. The querent or someone near her experiences deep unfolding, expansion, stretching.

The femaleness of the human species is suggested in the card and the passing of power from mother to daughter. The suggestion is that the female rightfully controls the size and character of the human species. Thus the querent may be faced with the reality of male control of female bodies, e.g., abortion rights, forced sterilization, prostitution, marriage, rape, incest.

Traditional meaning:

Fertility, sensuality, productivity. The mother figure representing abundance. Ishtar, Demeter/Kore, Aphrodite, the Corn Woman. The maternal aspect of the Triple Goddess, as the Priestess in her veiled or maiden aspect.

Reversed: BARRENNESS

Loss of resources. No creative thoughts. Lack of physical reproduction of any kind. A period of drought or famine. Temporary loss of ability to produce.

The querent or one near her cannot grow at this time. Systems seem to stop, or to carry forward by force of inertia alone. An important loss of some physical ability, perhaps only temporary. Possibility of death on some level.

The reversed card also suggests the barrenness visited by Demeter upon the earth out of revenge on man for the kidnap and rape of the daughter. Perhaps a deliberate refusal on the querent's part or on the part of one near her to bear the sons of man.

Traditional reversed meaning:

Sterility, dissipation of material resources. Loss, poverty. Maternal tyranny. Kali or Hecate, the vengeful mother.

4
THE EMPEROR
(Sign Aries)

THE EMPEROR.

Upright: DOMINATION

The archetypical king, the active father force, god-the-father, the ultimate patriarch. He is seated on stone in front of blood red mountains, reminders of the violence that his reign requires; animal skulls adorn his throne. Power-over, hierarchy, law—all institutionalized and called "natural," and "inevitable."

Circumstances are essentially out of the control of the querent and in the hands of male powers—the males in her life, the institutionalized powers of the patriarchy, the male qualities in herself or in others. She is subject to him, submissive to his dominance. This is also the card of controlled and blocked emotions; affect is gained if at all through physical sexuality.

It may be appropriate for the querent to behave in authoritative ways; she may be able to prevent her own victimization only by fighting back with the weapons of the oppressor, projecting and exercising power in a directive way. She may have to control by force someone or something and deal later with the consequences to her psyche.

Traditional meaning:

Power, authority, leadership. The domination of reason over emotion. Control, ambition. He who sets in order. Jehovah, Zeus, Thor.

Reversed: FANATICISM
(also Defeat)

Patriarchal powers become actively dangerous; some bursting of pressure points and the release of an uncontrolled power. The emperor has gone mad and a blood-bath threatens. Loss of control by somebody in a dominant power position.

The querent or one near her loses control of the dominant parts of herself and acts without reflection. She may be paranoid, temporarily unable to cope with reality. Her freak-out may require the support of a number of friends. Or, some power outside the querent breaks its traces to become an active and unpredictable threat to her, either physically or psychically.

The querent experiences a diminution of strength and a sense of defeat, drained by confrontation and struggle with the patriarchy—its agents externally, or its agents within her own psychic structure.

Traditional reversed meaning:

Weakness, lack of strength. Loss of control. Subservience to those in authority.

8

THE HIEROPHANT

5
THE HIEROPHANT
(Sign Taurus)

Upright: CONVENTIONALITY
(also Dogmatism)

The hierophant represents traditional or orthodox teaching; strict conformity to institutionalized rules and regulations; social approval; the ultimate in what-will-the-neighbors-think? Fear of disgrace; extreme pride in having the respect of others. The ritualistic, ceremonial, dramatic outer form; protocol, the ruling powers of the conventional.

For the querent, society or persons representing society, will not allow deviation; habit and social mores are of rising influence.

This card also represents those who want the world to be neat, schematic and orderly and who tend to be dogmatic about their beliefs, feeling that what they conceive to be right and truthful should be right and truthful for everyone else. Can be the card of the ideologue, the intellectual oppressor, the "correct liner," the inquisitor who seeks to eliminate deviation.

More positively the card suggests that the querent or one near her is a bridge, a translator, an interpreter, a teacher, as original hierophants were—showing the sacred reality to others, the door to the mysteries revealed by the High Priestess.

Traditional meaning:

Rule by the conventional, preference for the outer forms. Conformity. Intolerance, captivity to one's own ideas.

Reversed: REBELLION

Revolt against convention. Nonconformity, ingenious unorthodoxy. The pursuit of new ideas, alternative forms.

At the cost of deep pain the querent may break the icons, may stand free of some long-established convention. An ability to handle complexity, a tolerance for ambiguity, and a rejection of simplistic analysis and pat solutions.

Perhaps the mistaken destruction of some part of the system that could have been helpful. Throwing the baby out with the bathwater in a hasty action.

Traditional reversed meaning:

Unorthodoxy. Openness to new ideas. The card of the nonconformist.

6
THE LOVERS
(Sign Gemini)

Upright: MEANINGFUL
SEXUALITY
(also A Time of Choice)

THE LOVERS.

The man (conscious mind) looks to the woman (unconscious mind) as she and the angel exchange some knowledge. The suggestion is that any connection with "higher" or transcendent or cosmic energies must be through the unconscious. Woman has also traditionally been "body" so that to connect with the transcendent, consciousness must also transit the physical, particularly the sexual.

For the querent some question regarding sexuality or the physical. A love relationship carries deep meaning. Or there is sexual attraction outside a committed relationship. Questions of honesty and risk.

A card of harmony between body and mind, of the physical or material being invested with cosmic significance. Sexual expression. Lesbian lovemaking. Gay male or heterosexual intercourse carrying deep meaning. Meaningful autoeroticism.

The card also suggests a choice in the area of sexuality: between sexual expression which satisfies outward norms and that which provides self-fulfillment; to choose to love without obligation or restriction.

Traditional meaning:

A time of choice. The beginning of romance, love, harmony.

Reversed: DEGRADATION OF SEXUALITY
(also Wanting to Eat Your Cake and Have It Too)

Sexuality or physical expression modeled on power, on dominance-submission patterns. May speak to the nature of a whole relationship. Unfortunate choice of sexual expression, of partners, or of sexual experience. Jealousy, possessiveness, infidelity, romance. Superficial or unfulfilling love experiences.

An inability to make choices through wanting to have the best of all worlds, as in the woman who makes sexual choices incongruent with her true feelings.

The querent or one near her may be using sexual expression as a means to an end, or manipulating through sexual tactics. Sexual game-playing.

Traditional reversed meaning:

Infidelity, temptation. Frustration in love or marriage. The danger of a wrong choice in emotional relationships.

10

THE CHARIOT.

7
THE CHARIOT
(Sign Cancer)

Upright: WILL POWER

The charioteer has control of the chariot drawn by two figures: that is, control of the dual nature of the self. She is at a place of rest in her personal life which allows concentration on external affairs. The absence of reins and the presence of moon and stars surrounding her head suggest a psychic or psychological control of forces.

Some victory through personal effort and determination. Some battle of sheer will has been won; some habit broken; some seemingly impossible task of self-discipline accomplished. Progress in life is secure.

The querent or one near her is challenged by self-discipline or has accomplished it in some specific task. Or, the querent may be reminded of an addictive personality (hers or another's) and the need for will power or commitment in a change of habits. The card could indicate a conflict between two major forces in the querent's life.

Traditional meaning:

Control over health, money problems, enemies. Triumph through personal effort. The card of those who achieve greatness.

Reversed: LACK OF SELF-DISCIPLINE

The possibility of dissipation, decadence, insecurity, excessive pleasures, ill health. An addiction to some indulgence. Delay in self-knowledge; waste of personal resources.

The querent or one near her is not taking herself seriously, not caring for herself or disciplining herself. At this time there is a need for her to do that.

Or, some crisis may cause the querent to lower her defenses. She may lapse into old habits or tendencies, fall back on tools of survival that were learned early, e.g., she may move toward a patriarchal religious form or rely on violence or drugs in frustration with her life.

Traditional reversed meaning:

Conquered, overwhelmed. Decadent desires. Riding roughshod over others to achieve one's goals.

8
STRENGTH
(Sign Leo)

STRENGTH.

Upright: COURAGE

The woman stroking the animal suggests that power and dominion are not the issue at all—at least as conceived by the patriarchy. The strength shown here is not so much a matter of "taming" the "lower nature" so much as bridging spirit (person) and body (lion), relating to non-human forms in caring ways and working with nature and the material world. Strength comes not from the discipline of inner weakness (as with the Chariot) but from steadfast adherence to a principle or from strength of inner .conviction and harmony with the natural world. As with the Magician, the halo of infinity suggests connectedness and the lion, as the bridge between the human and the rest of nature, underscores that sense of connectedness.

Harmony between forces; stroking, caring, channeling healing energy. Triumph of love over strife, of concern over hate.

Courage on the querent's part makes possible some daring move toward caring; a risk, a reaching out to some person, thing, animal or plant. The courage which allows risk-taking. The querent or one near her may need the sustenance that relating to animals can give. Or the card may represent a cry for help directed at the querent from imprisoned or tortured animals.

Traditional meaning:

The triumph of love over hate. The courage of convictions. Reconciliation with an enemy. The defeat of base impulses.

Reversed: ALIENATION
(also Lack of Conviction)

Discord, strife with nature and materiality. Even cruelty to or neglect of animals or particular animal friends. Not enough attention to surroundings, to little things. Disjointed attempts to conquer material or animal worlds. A lack of relatedness to nature or to people thus allowing the objectification of them, perhaps even their victimization.

Refusal to risk caring. Continued isolation. Possible ill health.

The querent is distanced from herself; she perhaps constructs complex justifications (as with nuclear power) for her misuse of the earth and its creatures.

Traditional reversed meaning:

Weakness; a failure of nerve; lack of faith. Fear of the unknown in ourselves.

12

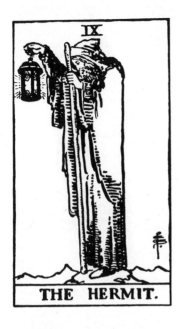

THE HERMIT.

9
THE HERMIT
(Sign Virgo)

Upright: SELF-SEARCH

The hermit has been alone on the silent white mountains of abstract thought. He has carried with him the lantern by which others may be guided to their own wisdom. He both seeks and has found; he has the sense of having been found. He is without arrogance or egotism.

The querent or one near her encounters the expert seeker and giver of intellect, knowledge, learning, the teacher of the meaning of both silence and sound. Possibly a journey to get to the teacher.

Also an indication that withdrawal for study and contemplation may be necessary. A time in which thought has priority over action, so that action will be sound. The querent may discover the need to look into the self, search for the self.

Traditional meaning:

Wisdom is offered. Silent counsel. Discretion, vigilance.

Reversed: DILETTANTISM

Wisdom is rejected. The querent shies away from solitude, knowledge of sound and silence. Or perhaps these things are inappropriate to the querent's life at this time.

Patent rejection of some patriarchal learning which may have some virtue.

Dilettantism or superficial knowledge. Buckshot learning. Skimming the surface.

The querent may need to pass completely through the "hero" stage before becoming the hermit. There is still action to be taken. No time yet for retreat or reflection.

Traditional reversed meaning:

Imprudence, foolishness, immaturity. Reliance on one's own inadequate knowledge when advice is offered.

13

10
THE WHEEL OF FORTUNE
(Planet Jupiter)

Upright: GOOD LUCK
(also Karmic Law)

External forces over which there is no direct control influence daily living. The cycles of an individual's life move without the will of the person involved. Coincidence. All the querent can do is be aware, try to understand what is happening, and roll with the punches.

The card can also suggest change in general rather than forces entirely outside the querent's control. Thus her own actions may become operative factors which determine or help to determine the turning of the wheel; she will receive the rewards of her labors, the fruits of her former deeds. She will reap what she sows.

The quaternary signs of the bull, lion, eagle, angel (symbols of earth, fire, air and water) represent the psychological functions of feeling, intellection, emotion and intuition. These must be balanced if the querent is to understand the turning of the wheel.

For the querent, new and more creative opportunities for growth.

Traditional meaning:

Unexpected turn of luck. The beginning of a new cycle in one's affairs. Whether good or bad depends on the surrounding cards—although usually the card means something positive.

Reversed: BAD LUCK

Some misfortune or downward turn of events; an unexpected setback in some enterprise or a change of conditions into something more challenging.

For the querent a period of opposition, frustration or a demand for extra energy, for attention to some particular problem or affair. Adversities which the querent must suffer until the wheel has turned full cycle.

Perhaps some inability in the querent to understand the movement of life, how changes occur on so many levels, often suddenly, to influence the whole.

Traditional reversed meaning:

Setbacks, bad breaks, irreversible adversities. Unexpected outside influences which do not help matters.

11
JUSTICE
(Sign Libra)

Upright: BALANCE

This mother goddess figure sits upon stone to dispense equity, but not patriarchal justice (whose standard is external action); she does the delicate balancing which weighs motive, circumstances, internal qualities. Psychologically the card suggests balance of circumstances, creative energy investments. On the external plane it refers to the kind of balance achieved by a small person, whose agility and centeredness allow her to defend herself against a larger enemy.

Justice will be done according to the querent's integrity and her understanding of justice. Some legal matter may be settled favorably, or an internal conflict may find resolution. There is the proper mixture of elements in a given circumstance, relationship or enterprise. What seems right or fair is happening. Nothing seems out of kilter or overweighted. The conflict is "clean."

Often an indication that some large social injustice is being altered, set right; or, on a personal scale, responding to another by giving them what they need.

Traditional meaning:

Fairness, reasonableness. The card can be positive or negative depending on the moral position of the querent. Balance is required.

Reversed: IMBALANCE

Some injustice, inequity or complication in a legal matter; perhaps bureaucratic red tape fouls up some process.

Perhaps a period of social injustices that outrage the human spirit. Sometimes the unbalanced presence of male energy. Some threat may soon emerge from "male" places (lodges, armies, fraternal orders, government, churches).

A lack of internal balance, an unwarranted emphasis upon one quality to the exclusion of another. Off center, out of kilter, flying off or being splattered over the horizon.

The querent feels justice is not being done or that her own internal world is askew.

Traditional reversed meaning:

Unfairness. Imbalance. Severity in judgement. Legal tangles.

12
THE HANGED MAN
(Planet Neptune)

THE HANGED MAN.

Upright: SUSPENSION
(also Transition)

A snare has caught up the androgynous figure to arrest him in his ordinary task. The figure is made powerless, made to surrender, made to listen to himself until he is set free. The expression on the figure's face indicates that the experience is not painful. On the contrary seeing the world from upside-down seems to have produced an ecstatic mood.

A pause in the querent's life for evaluation and/or perspective. Decisions should not be made now. Motion/activity should rest.

The Hanged Man also represents the sacrificial victim (the Green Man, the Winter King) who must die to ensure regeneration. The card therefore suggests the sacrifice of the male principle and the regeneration, reassertion of the female principle.

This is a card of the greatest strength.

Traditional meaning:

A pause in one's life. A reversal of one's way of life. Self-surrender to higher wisdom. A willingness to submit oneself to the dictates of the inner self. Regeneration, rebirth.

Reversed: SPEED
(also Stasis)

Driven behavior; speeding onward without pause and without awareness of danger. Reluctance to reflect. Much motion to no effect. Wheel-spinning inertia. May also be a gathering of momentum, not yet out of control. Excessive drive, action; imminent burn-out.

The male principle is running rampant, endangering female functioning and fertility.

The querent or one near her is absorbed in matters as yet unreflected upon. They threaten to run away with her.

Preoccupation with ego blocks growth in self-awareness. An inner struggle ends without progress being achieved.

Traditional reversed meaning:

Absorption in materialism. Going with the crowd. Avoidance of spiritual growth.

DEATH.

13
DEATH
(Sign Scorpio)

Upright: CHANGE AND RENEWAL

A "busy" card, packed with a juxtaposition of symbols. Clearly the figure of Death has the power that there is not standing against—whether king or commoner, old or young, man or woman, priest or layperson.

A protest against stagnation. The end of something (often of the personal view) and the beginning of something new (of the cosmic or universal view). More often it is the unviolent death of some status quo which in turn makes way for new ideas, situations, people, opportunities, possibilities.

The querent will experience more than the usual change in her daily life, particularly in the realm of consciousness and values.

Traditional meaning:

Change, transformation, renewal. Destruction which has a positive outcome—clearing the way for change. One removes what is outdated and superfluous from one's life.

Reversed: INERTIA
(also Stagnation)

An indication that whatever is happening will continue to happen. A feeling of no growth, no activity, either inner or outer. Stagnation. Deepening ennui.

The querent's life is not changing at this time. A relationship may be being taken for granted. The essentials of life may be assured. The systems that support the querent are intact, the values unquestioned. Things may not necessarily be quiet, but simply unchanging in pattern.

The querent may criticize herself unnecessarily for failing to move but in fact probably what she is doing she needs to be doing; if she needed to be doing something else, she would be doing that.

Traditional reversed meaning:

Stagnation, immobility, inertia, lethargy, petrifaction. Political upheaval and revolution (the King trampled underfoot)—remember, this is bad from the point of view of most traditional interpreters.

14
TEMPERANCE
(Sign Sagittarius)

Upright: INTEGRATION

The angel pours the stuff of life back and forth from the unconscious to the conscious. Vibrations and radiant energy temper experience just as pouring back and forth creates the liquid. Here it is the act, the motion, of integration that is important. As an individual or as a social entity it is time to pay attention consciously to certain experiences—to pour them back and forth that they may be re-energized, re-understood, given new meaning.

Time for the querent or one near to reflect, to integrate, to bring oneself into balance, to straighten out the priorities of one's life. Harmony and cooperation are called for or are imminent.

The card's natural setting suggests a rare harmony of the human with earth, trees, water, animals. The querent needs to touch this harmony, be reminded of it lest her activities scatter her, alienate her from "home."

The card suggests moderation, economy in the expenditure of energy, a balance of external activities with inward reflection.

Traditional meaning:

Harmonization, coordination, accommodation, mixing. Successful union, fusion, bringing together.

Reversed: FRAGMENTATION

Attention to experience is not now necessary. Life can be sustained for a while without deliberate efforts to integrate. More input is possible without reflection. But fragments of experience cannot remain too long unattended or they will claim attention in explosive ways.

The querent is in a period of activity, of external and probably fast-moving functioning. There is no danger at this time or need now to stop and assess. For a while fragmentation is tolerable.

The card may also hint that some inability to work with others is blocking achievement. Groups or individuals that thought they could work together effectively do not "mix" after all.

Traditional reversed meaning:

Disunion, quarreling, inability to work with others. Conflicts of interest, competing interests.

THE DEVIL .

15
THE DEVIL
(Sign Capricorn)

Upright: BONDAGE

The chains on both figures are removable at will. They link the figures to the throne of material immediacy, that is to the experience of life without the sense of history or association. Sensation divorced from understanding.

There are parts of the querent or of a social/political situation surrounding her which are not yet understood on any level. They are buried deep. They need to be placed within an historical context and their associations made clear.

The corruption of the early Pan figure (or the satyr) into the evil devil is a Judeo-Christian embellishment that aids the notion that all of nature is "less" than mankind and thus in need of taming.

The chains are habits forged of unreflected-upon happenings where the querent has been the unconscious agent or victim—essentially a self-limitation. An oppressive circumstance, not yet recognized, understood, or even felt as pain. Resignation, depression which, if the querent only knew it, are easily thrown off.

Traditional meaning:

Self-destructiveness. Bondage to the material. Subordination. Evil, sadism, weird experience.

Reversed: RECOGNITION OF BONDAGE

Desire for freedom from some unconscious or unacknowledged painful condition. The present is seen in perspective and is linked with the totality of the querent's experience. A circumstance is understood, a habit broken. Something thought to have been "choice" is understood to have been "conditioning."

The querent or someone near her understands some aspect of the self that has chained her to a destructive practice. There may be some breakthrough in sexual experience or in the understanding of violence. A reconciliation with time, perhaps even with death. A vision of release.

Traditional reversed meaning:

Release from bondage. Overcoming the fear of one's own self. The beginning of understanding.

16
THE TOWER
(Planet Mars)

THE TOWER.

Upright: VIOLENT REVOLUTION (also Overthrow of False Consciousness)

Violent social conflict and change; destruction of the old order on a grand scale. Release from imprisonment in one of the patriarchal towers as it is demolished. Its fortifications no longer exist; it no longer defends and keeps surveillance. Its dungeons are emptied. Freedom is won at a high cost.

The querent may suffer bankruptcy, disruption of a career, loss of a job, of a power position. More likely there will be the overthrow of some institution or an entire social order.

Violence is triggered by repression or lack of opportunity to reflect. Unleashed rage occurs without regard for consequences.

Violent overthrow inside the querent which could occur in a flash of illumination. The querent may undergo a sudden change of ideas, values; a rapid, painful mental transition or raising of consciousness. The sudden conversion.

May be the shattering of a relationship. But since the change usually involves the overthrow of false values and beliefs the new consciousness (the altered condition) is ultimately liberating.

Traditional meaning:

A sudden change of beliefs. Disruption which brings enlightenment. The destruction of an outdated philosophy. Unforeseen catastrophe.

Reversed: SLOW CHANGE (also False Consciousness)

Continued oppression with no overthrow in sight. Small changes only are underway. A concerted and far-reaching effort on the part of a great many people to create social change. Very little dramatic action. Or no significant change at all. The haves continue to have, the have-nots to have not. Gradual deterioration of circumstances.

Or, change in the querent is blocked through adherence to an outmoded belief system, or because of a rigid dogmatism. Perhaps she is denying her pain.

Traditional reversed meaning:

Stuck in the rut of old values. An inability to bring about change. Freedom achieved after heavy struggle. False imprisonment, accusations.

THE STAR.

17
THE STAR
(Sign Aquarius)

Upright: HEALING

Waterbearer (here, the Great Mother as Isis-Urania) kneels in astral light to stir up the pool of the unconscious. She refreshes herself with water, drenches the earth with it. She gives sustenance to herself and to materiality itself. She bathes herself as well in lifegiving radiant cosmic energy. She is open to all lifegiving forces that well up from within. A healing that is achieved through dipping into the unconscious and listening to the inner voices.

A rural setting where stars can be seen. The card suggests a healthy environment free from pollution and exploitation, psychic or material, the kind of environment that creates healthy people. The querent may need to take action to preseve nature or her own health, especially through meditation. Or the querent or someone close to her has an experience of increased good health—physical and/or mental. Perhaps a charging of the energy batteries through water or starshine or through some more unexpected source. She feels *good*.

Traditional meaning:

Hope, inspiration, bright prospects. Widening horizons. New life and vigor. A very favorable card.

Reversed: ILL HEALTH
(also Pessimism)

Some cut-off from life-giving sources. Malaise, lack of energy doldrums, fatigue. Perhaps an experience of mental illness. Fear of opening to the sources of health. Tightness. Some alienation from the unconscious, or from understanding it.

Self-doubt which narrows the querent's outlook and constricts her belief in her life possibilities. Perhaps she must armor against an enemy.

The reversed card may be a warning against western or allopathic medicine (the traumatic treatment of symptoms). It suggests that the whole body, the whole environment must create health. The querent or one near her may be threatened by male or patriarchal interference in her physical life. A harsh and perhaps unnecessary alternative may be forced upon her body in the name of "health."

Traditional reversed meaning:

Self-doubt. Unfulfilled hope. Illness. Pessimism.

18
THE MOON
(Sign Pisces)

THE MOON.

Upright: INTUITION

In the light of the Moon the querent exposes her catch, her harvest, from the pool of the unconscious. Primitive and perilous thoughts emerge from the Water-Bearer's pool—now in the foreground—with the center of interest focused on the distant mountains of thought, where the querent may find consciousness and integration. But the towers of patriarchy are intact, and life is blocked by having to enter through that gateway. As she rains energy upon them (the Yods), the Moon liberates the path.

The power of psychic endowment—dreams, intuition, hunches—confront the fears which are embedded in the unconscious, placed there early on by socialization and enculturation. The querent or one near her will make a major break-through to freedom and integration if she opens herself to her psychic powers. Her relationship to her inner powers changes. She finds support for her unpopular ideas or grows in her own convictions.

There is some freeing of restriction. Socially some liberation or reform.

A revolt of the natural against artificial forces. Some breaking loose or breaking through of the earth or the environment. Elements that have been harnessed are released.

Traditional meaning:

Intuition, the power of the instincts. Deception, hidden enemies, darkness. Dread of the irrational.

Reversed: OBSTRUCTED INTUITION

The peril in the card, particularly reversed, is in the towers, in their obstruction of natural forces. The animal-like, the oppressed, are impelled by the moon to howl against the artificial, the super-imposed, the oppressive. Psychic powers are limited.

The querent or one near her is frustrated by limitations on the intuitive. If she stays in touch with inner intelligences she may yet pass through the patriarchal gateway to a place of wholeness.

The card may suggest mistreatment or misuse of a woman or of nature; a violation, a rape, an imprisonment.

Traditional reversed meaning:

Deception and danger to a lesser degree. Imagination is curbed by the demands of the practical world.

THE SUN.

19
THE SUN
(Planet Sun)

Upright: REBIRTH

A big turn in the journey toward the self or toward new forms of art and intellectual expression. Some union of the conscious with unconscious brings about the rebirth of a new whole: a new person, a new society, or new values. The red banner of action is also the versatile costume for the theatre (the let's-pretend of artistic transformation). The child relates to the horse and the sunflowers through psychic channels. She addresses the world with the same spirit of play and optimism that the Fool exhibits. But she has lived more than the Fool, and the play is out of a more authentic experience.

For the querent something new and of deep significance in her life. A successful change testifying to an integration after stormy (revolutionary) times. Pain is largely behind now or can be dealt with more creatively. Joyful affirmation of existence.

The card can suggest the affirmation of a physical baby or child.

Traditional meaning:

Success generally. Happiness of all kinds: emotional, material, creative, social. Glory, abundant joy.

Reversed: CLINGING

The delay of rebirth. Clinging to the painful struggle out of fear of letting go or fear of death. Energy cannot be freed for the movement to new life.

The querent or one near her is resisting death or change. It may not be time for the new. External circumstances may be too perilous to allow anything but bare survival, hanging on.

May be a loss of spirit or of the impulse to transform. Artistic enterprises may be arrested.

Traditional reversed meaning:

Arrogance, display, vanity. Future plans clouded. The same happiness, only in a lesser degree.

20
JUDGEMENT
(Planet Pluto)

JUDGEMENT.

Upright: BEYOND JUDGEMENT
(also Re-Awakening)

The completion and ending of all judgement as we have experienced it. Perhaps a shedding of high competitive standards for the self—the end of self-judgement and comparisons with others as well as the end to societal definitions or standards for judging or condemning.

Differences (qualities, quantities, actions) are raised up from the sarcophagi to be judged "lesser" or "greater" for the last time. Self-definition follows immediately. The swansong—played by the patriarchal angel from on high—of the external standards of definition and identification.

The querent experiences an awakening from her own self-hatred, guilt, or penance. Judgements from others no longer have any meaning. A card of initiation into a new plane of awareness, new dimensions in consciousness. Putting new life into deadened feelings; revitalizing one's life.

Traditional meaning:

Judgement, the final determination of something with the suggestion of something to follow. Resurrection, choice, initiation.

Reversed: PERSISTENCE OF JUDGEMENT

Continuing to judge by external standards. Heavy negative self-criticism and guilt orgies. Conventional acceptance of hierarchical values and the right to judge others.

The querent or one near her flees from judgement, at the same time levelling heavy self-criticism. Part of her fear of death, perhaps, and the judgement the culture assures her will be awaiting her after death.

The querent may become a professional judge of others (a teacher, a supervisor, etc.); she may struggle with that role.

Traditional reversed meaning:

Fear of death. Reluctance to reach conclusions. Failure to find happiness.

THE WORLD.

21
THE WORLD
(Planet Saturn)

Upright: COMPLETION

The satisfactory completion of some cycle. An enterprise accomplished. The four balanced corners (the archetypical creatures) and the circular wreath indicate that the end of an era has arrived. All details are accounted for and nothing extraneous interferes. A short period of stability before a new movement begins.

The theatrical banner of transformation suggests that now creativity may take place in earnest. The dancer and her twirling batons are framed in a complete picture of performance.

Or perhaps the querent can cease playing roles and settle in with a more consistent identity, and harmonize the different parts of the self.

Traditional meaning:

Synthesis, crystallization. Perfection, cosmic consciousness. The path of liberation.

Reversed: INCOMPLETION

An incomplete state, but leaning toward completion. Frustration at the inability to finish some important task. A deliberate (perhaps unconscious) hanging on to prevent some ending.

The querent or one near her has not yet reached a point of closure on a part of her life's cycle. Things are still indecisive regarding some enterprise, perhaps in her schooling or training. Much unexplained. Much still pending.

A performance is incomplete, perhaps interrupted. Or a performance is in jeopardy—the querent does not know her lines or she has not practiced or she is not in shape for an upcoming demand on her body and on her creativity. She may be fearing to be embarassed before peers—or before followers, or before those who will judge her on the completion or wholeness of her work.

Traditional reversed meaning:

Lack of vision blocks success. Inertia, stubbornness, clinging to old habits and habits resist change.

The Minor Arcana

The Pentacles

THE SUIT OF PENTACLES

(Earth, physical sensation, money, acquisition, trade. The suit of the worker, the businessperson.)

This suit speaks of the practical ways that the material world functions for us in our creativity and self-expression. It is the suit of work, of craftship and art, of career and material possessions. It speaks more of material than of spiritual opulence, more of material than of spiritual poverty, even though through the awareness of creativity it allows for the existence of the psychic; in some places it specifically evokes images of psychic power (the page and the queen).

For the most part the pentacles speak in terms of possession and earned goods and services, of the world as the generation(s) immediately before us have known it, and not so much of what it suggests of art and creativity and of the liberating function of meaningful work is applicable to any society. Pentacles is coin—competition and even war—but also an expression of the use of cooperation and creativity.

Like the suit of cups, pentacles have to do with the querent's *perception* and *understanding* rather than with her *judgements* and *actions* (the function of the suits of swords and wands). The pentacles suggest ways of perceiving the "real" world of "things" and allow for understanding that world without the necessity of evaluation or judgement.

ACE ♣ PENTACLES

ACE OF PENTACLES

Upright: **THE GIFT OF PRODUCTIVITY**
(also Prosperity)

The ace represents the source or the center of power, that place where power's presence is most intensely felt. The well-spring. In this case the source is of creative or acquisitive power. An unimpeded flow of productive energy.

The querent or one near her is assured of her potential to produce artifacts or to acquire material goods. There is even the strong possibility of wealth. The path invites her beyond the security of the formal garden into the landscape where things may be more risky. The querent or one near her may already have attained material or artistic success.

The card may be a promise only: that work can be meaningful, that talent is present, that the world will receive the querent's work.

Traditional meaning:

Perfection, prosperity, attainment, ecstasy. Contentment, security, appreciation of the good things of life. According to Waite, the most favorable of the minor arcana.

Reversed: REFUSAL OF THE GIFT OF GAIN
(also Materialistic Attitudes)

The gift may never be offered, but more likely, it is offered and turned down: perhaps out of lack of desire for financial or creative gain, perhaps out of political motives, perhaps out of experience of false starts and capricious dealings.

In the reverse the card is not an advantageous one in terms of worldly wealth. Too much greed or dependence on material well-being on the part of the querent may lead to riches but without fulfillment. Perhaps the card warns that financial or creative power has dire consequences if it is not grounded in a regard for the earth, the environment.

Can also represent misused wealth.

Traditional reversed meaning:

Prosperity without happiness. Dependence on physical pleasures for happiness. Corruption by wealth.

TWO OF PENTACLES

Upright: MANIPULATION

The juggler is a real operator, both of human beings and of material goods/ services. The ability to balance one deal, one person, against another, usually in a gameful or clever way. An ingenious, charming individual of high business acumen; the low key but manipulative salesperson; a circumstance that calls for a delicate balancing of resources. Perhaps also, in a more positive sense, the ability to juggle simultaneously several projects or to work toward several goals at once. An individual who works alone trusting no one. The figure could become the king of pentacles.

Not an evil person, but one who has learned well the rules of the game and lives by the charming use of people. The card may represent the querent or one near her, or parts of the querent. The card also suggests a state of vacillation.

Travel, messages, commerce are hinted at by the ships. The juggler has far-reaching enterprises.

Traditional meaning:

Knowledgeable manipulation of the rules of life. The ability to juggle two situations at the same time. Fun and recreation.

Reversed: SHAM DISCOVERED (also Instability)

Desperation or even chicanery is revealed beneath the confident exterior. Some breakdown in the querent's usual charm and ability at handling personal or commercial situations. Mock gaiety no longer conceals the manipulation. Perhaps the manipulator is becoming more honest. Perhaps some admission of the need for other people or relief at no longer having to dissemble.

Misfortune because of lack of balance or because circumstances cannot be balanced. The juggling act comes apart.

Traditional reversed meaning:

Unstable effort. Inability to carry through ideas/projects. Inconsistency of action which endangers success. Enforced gaiety.

THREE OF PENTACLES

Upright: SKILLS ON THE MARKETPLACE (also Establishment Approval)

Marketing some intellectual or creative skill to an established institution as suggested by the artisan displaying her work for the approval of church officials. The craftsperson, having completed some artwork or finished her technical/intellectual/artistic training now puts herself out for approval to those who may buy her skills. Possible feelings of creative prostitution, or simply concern about the reception of one's work and the judgement of the external world.

Deep questions of integrity versus political expedience attend this card; the danger is that need might force capitulation to or compromise with an order that holds down people with differences from the mainstream.

The querent or someone close to her is called to sell her wares; she probably will do it and pay a price for it.

In a more neutral sense making a commitment to, putting one's energies into a major project.

Traditional meaning:

Praise or appreciation from someone already established in one's area of work. Or, establishment approval and critical praise.

Reversed: SKILLS UNMARKETED

Refusal to market wares or skills either because it seems a prostitution or because the querent fears success, responsibility or criticism. Perhaps the querent's skills are insufficient to be marketed; she may lack ability to excel at her chosen work.

Possibly just criticism of creative work by those respected in that field.

The institution does not get the skill or the product; that may be immediately or ultimately unfortunate for the querent or one associated with her. Perhaps some purity of product is maintained by the refusal to market it.

Traditional reversed meaning:

Lack of skill. Mediocrity; commonplace ideals. Sloppiness. Conceit which prevents one from listening to the advice of others more skilled.

33

FOUR OF PENTACLES

Upright: MISERLINESS

The miser, the person who has made moderate material or artistic gains, clings to her possessions without sharing. Social amnesia. Forgetting the group, particularly family or cultural ties. Individualism. The figure clings to all her gains; to people, too, making them her possessions and sharing very little of money or emotion.

May be material or elite artistry or hoarded technical knowledge on the querent's part or on the part of one near her.

The attempt to achieve power through the acquisition of goods and wealth without regard to changes needed in the system. The consumer mentality. Looking for security by piling up possessions, or, hanging onto what has provided security in the past—people, values, circumstances.

Traditional meaning:

A miserly, ungenerous character. Cleaving to that which one has. Material gain, inheritance.

Reversed: EXTRAVAGANCE

Generosity to a fault. Probably misuse of money, possessions, knowledge, gifts, skills. The spendthrift with all resources, often giving them when they are not asked for or needed—sometimes when they are not wanted.

A tendency to try to impress people with material possessions; the attempt to buy respect and status with large expenditures. Perhaps the querent or one near her shows off her power or her goods in the face of those that she has risen above.

The querent may too readily give her energy and attention to other people, thus spreading herself too thin.

Traditional reversed meaning:

The spendthrift. Loss or setbacks in the material sphere.

FIVE OF PENTACLES

Upright: POVERTY

Physical deprivation. Hunger. Disease. Defeat. Being left out in the cold. Or, the fear of these things. The consequences of lack of money. The querent or one near her may suffer a setback in money. Or if the querent is inside looking out, some recognition of poverty may change her life.

On the creative level the refusal of institutions to take seriously the querent's abilities. Rejection of her work or her manner of self-expression. Only by the standards of the institutions themselves are skills presently judged—and too often found lacking.

Also the possibility that the querent is voluntarily giving up something of value—voluntarily experiencing hardship—to break through to something new.

Traditional meaning:

Unemployment, destitution, severe material adversity.

Reversed: ALTERNATIVES

The figures in the snow may find others similarly victims. Enough shared pain can become revolutionary rage. Important bonds may be forged with those sharing the same plight. There are alternatives to be found. Seen in this way, the reversed card provides a connection to the suit of wands, the suit that suggests revolutionary political action.

Rejection of the forces that create poverty. Action at a grass-roots level to form coalitions. A time for political organizing or alternative structures. New interest in political matters on the querent's part. Self-education into consciousness. Focusing rage into action. The querent's survival is temporarily assured.

Traditional reversed meaning:

New employment. Money obtained through hard work. Charity.

SIX OF PENTACLES

Upright: CONDESCENSION
(also Philanthropy)

The successful person on the way up commercially, in moderate or comfortable circumstances. Condescension on her part toward those who are still where she once was.

The querent or someone near her is in danger of forgetting her roots, of denying her culture or upbringing. She is trying to forget her obligation to overthrow the system. She gives charity to those who remind her of that obligation. Tokenism. A bending of the system to keep the lid on discontent by giving the bare necessities of survival.

The querent or one influencing her is probably "fair" and may believe herself to be a reformist. But though she may once have had the commitment to make things better for people like herself, she is now deeply bought by the system.

The querent may be in the role of begger for favors. She may be called upon to swallow her distaste of the role and receive help from someone offering to help.

More positively, the querent gives away or shares something in which she is well-endowed—energy, knowledge, skills.

Traditional meaning:

Charity, sympathy, sharing with others. You will get what you deserve.

Reversed: CLASS LOYALTY

Genuine sharing of newly-gained wealth and skills with those still oppressed. Or the querent or one near her may refuse to buy into the system even though she has the chance.

Perhaps the refusal to beg from or demean herself before another. Questions may arise around taking "dirty" money.

Most likely the querent or someone close is struggling to recognize and overcome her condescension and class denial.

Traditional reversed meaning:

The misuse of money. Purse-proud. Gifts given, but from selfish motives.

SEVEN OF PENTACLES

Upright: ANXIETY ABOUT PRODUCE

A period of self-evaluation of one's productivity. The figure has planted and it looks like there is to be a good crop but the harvest is not yet ready. Some doubt exists about the possibility of marketing the crop. It seems much work for little gain. Sheer survival may be at stake: where to find a job, how to get trained for productive work.

A person attempting to express work and the creative urge in some way close to the earth or out of some natural or primary (not intermediary) source. Not an interpreter but a creator, close to raw materials in making something. Yet dependent for a livelihood on productivity. Hence the anxiety and concern.

The possibility that productive efforts made in the past may be wasted by inaction in the present; or that productive efforts in the past are yielding results too slowly. In both cases, the anxiety is misplaced.

Traditional meaning:

Money worries, specifically about a loan. Speculations that don't pay off. Pause during the growth of an enterprise.

Reversed: PROCESS-MANIA

Easing of anxiety about work, however difficult. A sense of worth through the work itself with minimal regard for the livelihood to be provided by the harvest. Perhaps foolhardiness in this respect; no sense of product but obsession with the joy of process. Often not very practical. The querent or one near her takes no thought for the morrow, fails to see or understand the need for a product.

The querent or one near may need some shaking into hard reality.

Traditional reversed meaning:

Impatience. Again, anxieties about money, investments, loans.

EIGHT OF PENTACLES

Upright: APPRENTICESHIP

A time of learning, practicing, getting skills ready for the world. Not yet an artisan. Growing, listening to others, taking suggestions, modelling after others with only occasional excursions into one's own creativity. Learning the craft; hands-on experience. Technical accomplishment; mastering the tools of a trade. Intellectual, artistic, psychic, psychological, political, physical or business powers are being developed. Concentrating on the development of one's craft or work.

There is the suggestion that the querent or one associated with her may be a person who never masters a trade perhaps because of lack of talent in that area, perhaps because the economic obstacles are too great.

Traditional meaning:

Skill in work (perhaps in the preparatory stage). Using skills in a way which is satisfactory and useful. A good card for anyone with talent.

Reversed: MEANINGLESSNESS
(also Aimlessness)

Lack of desire to learn or loss of kinship with one's creative powers. What-do-I-do-with-my-life? Perhaps existential *angst* with no drive to achieve marketable or even self-fulfilling skills. May signify meaningless work. Drudgery. Alienation from creativity, even forced labor.

The querent or one near feels inertia, lack of motivation to work (or to get out of meaningless work). Perhaps despair at the prospect of work within the present culture's values.

The card sometimes suggests the person with the sure-fire project that never materializes.

Traditional reversed meaning:

Misuse, dishonest use of skill. Misplaced vanity about one's work. Failing in one's work ambitions.

NINE OF PENTACLES

Upright: SOLITARY CREATIVITY

Creativity practiced in solitude, without others but with animals or other growing things; perhaps the desire for such solitude and privilege. No necessary involvement in the commercial nexus because the products of labor are themselves sustenance, or because circumstances are comfortable enough without money having to be an issue. Creations that do not necessarily go on the common market but that are enjoyed by a limited number of people. The Venus symbols suggest that she lives and is sustained by other women.

The querent or someone close to her is developing a special product/crop under special conditions. Both the grapes and the hooded falcon suggest the negative aspects of creativity fostered by privilege: the grapes hint at self-indulgence, the falcon of those who are exploited in order to provide privilege for the few.

More positively, simply taking pleasure in what one has produced or created on one's own.

Traditional meaning:

Material well-being. Solitary enjoyment of the good things in life (meaning without dependence on men?). Love of nature; success in growing things.

Reversed: COMMERCIALIZATION (Work in the Marketplace)

Co-option of a product or of an entire culture; commercialization of something precious, particularly one's personal rituals or ethnic conventions. Something better kept at low visibility among a few people is put on the market for material livelihood.

There is little or no opportunity for the solitary cultivation of creative powers. Lack of material resources make such a way of life impossible. A barrier to private self-expression and a forcing of it into a public sphere. Relinquishing the creative in order to survive.

Traditional reversed meaning:

Canceled project. Loss of home. A warning that present material well-being may not continue.

TEN OF PENTACLES

Upright: FAMILY TIES

The established and privileged patriarchal family carrying on its prosperity and its pride in tradition. The coat of arms and the dogs testify to the comfort of living in the manner approved of and supported by present social and economic structures. But not just an upperclass family. It may be an extended family or social unit whose values claim the querent's loyalty.

Moderate material wealth. Intense training of children both morally and practically in how to handle money. Perhaps an inheritance or some positive reaching out from the querent's family or from a family that the querent feels she could belong to.

Suggestion that the querent or one near could be restricted or benefited by family ties, family security, family comfort, depending on surrounding cards.

Traditional meaning:

Inheritance. Family wealth. Family affairs.

Reversed: FAMILY PRESSURE

Expectation of "appropriate" behavior come to the fore. Daughters or sons are called on to respond to standards of the group that brought them up.

Loss of money or approval from family. Some negative communication from such a group, usually of an economic nature or having to do with societal norms. Some recent or renewed pressure from old ties that the querent cast aside. A backlash against radical action. Seen in this way the card can be a connecting link to the suit of swords.

The querent may impose demands on herself to meet the need of a family member, usually at the cost of the querent's own well-being.

Traditional reversed meaning:

Family misfortune. The restricting effects of long tradition. Problems with elderly family members.

PAGE of PENTACLES.

PRINCESS OF PENTACLES
(Or Page)

Upright: INCREASING POWERS

Intellect, creativity, financial acumen being discovered or trained. The natural setting and the floating pentacle suggest that psychic powers are also developing; in this case they are connected with work and career, for example following the intuition in financial speculation. The card thus becomes a connecting one to the suit of cups.

Through lots of work—diligent scholarship, personal discipline, responsible analysis, the querent or someone close achieves entry into the economic world.

Or perhaps powers of accomplishment not yet used or even developed. Particularly psychic powers. A challenge to develop such powers.

Traditional meaning:

Good management, prudence, conscientiousness, diligence. A message of good news about a money matter.

Reversed: REPRESSED POWER

A hiding of gifts or a denial of them. Lack of cultivation of psychic or practical powers. Perhaps a keeping of important information, a secret. Possibly the misuse of the gifts of power in financial matters. Lack of awareness of potential, perhaps because economic position has never allowed proper exploration of talents or because the querent was discouraged from developing such talents. Likely a person of lower class or nondominant ethnic group whose powers have been subverted or denied.

Traditional reversed meaning:

Wastefulness, prodigality. Too meticulous; hampered by the mind-set of the petty bureaucrat. Bad news about money.

PRINCE OF PENTACLES
(Or Knight)

Upright: PRACTICALITY
(also Hard Work)

The mercenary soldier who deliberately extends her skills or labor for a
price and who limits her responsibility
to her paycheck's requirements. There is
no personal investment in or identification with or loyalty to the enterprise
of the employer but rather a practical
trade agreement to sell work for money.
Important pleasures come after hard
labor—drinking, socializing, hanging out.
She earns her way (secretary, manual
laborer, domestic worker, maybe even
management) and is often impatient with
those who don't (the lazy, the "free-
riders" on welfare).

The querent or one near her is not
associated with political struggle but
rather lives in a personal equilibrium
with the system, even though that system does not function in her own best
interests.

KNICHT of PENTACLES.

Also externalizing one's abilities, one's productive powers.

Traditional meaning:

A methodical, patient, responsible laborer who is the upholder of traditional values.
Unimaginative, she usually depends on established authority rather than exercising her
own judgement. "He rides a slow, enduring, heavy horse to which his own aspect corres-
ponds." (Waite)

Reversed: UNEARNED EASE
(also Inertia)

No visible source of income and yet never in want. Lucky investments.
Wild ideas work. Little effort seems always to pay off heavily, perhaps
through welfare scams.

The querent or one associated with her is something of a dilettante, often
wasteful with an abundance of seemingly natural gifts. Hard work seems unnecessary in her life. She always has people loving her, money coming into
the till, ideas enriching her life. Perhaps a manipulator of people who should
be warned that others' generosity has its limits. Perhaps to discipline her gifts
or to put them to work in a regular job would destroy her luck, she feels.

Traditional reversed meaning:

Inertia, idleness, lack of determination. Sloppiness, carelessness. Dull-witted and self-
righteous, she is the champion of an outmoded system against the forces of progress.

42

KING of PENTACLES

KING OF PENTACLES

Upright: MATERIAL SUCCESS

At the pinnacle of material power, ownership of vast properties. The capitalist. The corporate businessman or the government worker who has made the right corporate connections. He has fought his way up through the white fraternal system.

Perhaps sensual power as well as financial and even the hint of dissipation in the grapes that hang so abundantly about him. There is no questioning of the system on his part. Ease and charity. He will assure us that he helps his friends, that his wealth is used in beneficial ways, that anyone could have done what he did if only they had the perseverence.

Not so much a fanatic on law and order as the full-fledged patriarch. He does not have to be since he is totally secure. He invests. He proliferates his power and his pleasure.

He dwells in the querent's life somewhere or his characteristics are a part of the querent or one near her.

Traditional meaning:

An experienced and successful leader in business and industry. Enormous financial talents, mathematical gifts—great success in these paths. Reliability, steadiness.

Reversed: ECONOMIC NAIVETE

Little wealth, perhaps not even moderate wealth, though a constant striving to be wealthy and to enjoy the opulence of the successful financier. Lack of individual flair for monetary gain or in making the system work for one. Bafflement by money and economic principles. Or refusal to deal with material necessities; some freak-out around handling money.

The querent or one near her does not know how to make things work for herself either economically or in other practical circumstances. Frustrating ignorance in the face of others' continuing success.

The card suggests one who is a loser though always trying to pull off a big deal, even in spite of lack of skills.

Traditional reversed meaning:

A thriftless gambler. The use of any means to achieve financial success—vice, corruption, perversity (the pimp, the drug dealer). Servile, easily bought.

43

QUEEN OF PENTACLES

Upright: PHYSICALITY

The woman who has made it materially by the use of her physical body, perhaps in sports or dance but more likely in modeling, perhaps in prostitution. She might also be the ordinary well-off housewife who has been what she was told to be: beautiful, clever consort to her husband and bearer of his children. If so, then she has not been distanced from the natural elements that assure her a level of integration. She has probably made of her home a remarkable oasis of genuine love in a desert of alienated materiality. To the extent that she uses her body as "ground" for her accomplishments and creativity, she unites body and spirit, thus becoming a kind of bridge to the suit of cups.

The querent or one near has capitalized on those characteristics that define her as a woman: beauty, passion, even fertility. She has had a good relationship to her physical body and the use of it in self-expression, personal achievement and career. Her creations have been physical, lovemaking, children, sensual pleasure or physical comfort.

Traditional meaning:

The Empress, the earth mother, in her lesser arcana manifestation. A woman lavish with her affections. Wealthy, but with a generous and responsible attitude toward her money. Prosperity, abundance.

Reversed: BODY TENSION

Tightness of body and inability to relate to physicality. Perhaps a temporary condition made all the more painful by memories of ease or freedom. Tension or difficulty in sexual or physical circumstances. Tense response to everything.

The querent or one near her suffers from some hypertension that obstructs energy flow; she fails to connect body to spirit or mind. Lack of trust of her body. Or, the querent may have failed in beauty-passion-fertility-homemaking. She may have bought the feminine mystique or the romantic dream, all in vain.

Traditional reversed meaning:

A grasping person whose life is circumscribed by material possessions. One who surrounds herself with flatterers. Dependence on others. Fear of failure.

The Swords

THE SUIT OF SWORDS

(Air, reason, logic, ambition, aggression, conflict, competition. The suit of the patriarchy.)

In a positive sense the suit suggests the usefulness of logic and clarity, the virtue of clean severing of confused elements into separate entities so that each can be assessed in order and in relation to other parts; feminist strategy requires the acknowledgement of these sword-like qualities and affirms the proper use of reason.

Patriarchy, however, has made too much of reason, enthroning it above other faculties (feeling, intuitiion, sensation). This leads to a mindset that is destructive of life and the biosphere: competition, war, exploitation, power-over relationships, dependency, possessiveness, elitism, hierarchies, human chauvinism. It is the suit of the warrior, the suit of the dominant social orders, most exaggerated in Western Europe and the United States where it has been made to seem more palatable—even natural—through the virtues of capitalism and the glories of romance. But it represents patriarchy in any form, including the socialist systems where big brother has replaced big daddy. It broadly represents men, their rational power, their scientific method, and their strict socialization into the myth of their own superiority.

In this suit are all the vertical societal structures, the mystifications of the Judeo-Christian heritage, the institutions of oppression of all women, people of color and physically different people, and the mindset of power over others. More often than not swords must be read as aggression, fragmentation, strife, hatred, war, misfortune, disaster.

Like the suit of wands, swords have to do with the querent's *judgements* and *actions* rather than with *perceptions* and *understandings* (the functions of pentacles and cups). Swords offer reason as the discriminating faculty, the faculty of judgement. On the basis of that faculty swords suggest actions that tend to support the status quo, the patriarchal system. More often than not, the suit represents the misuse of reason rather than its best application.

ACE OF SWORDS

Upright: THE GIFT OF SOCIAL ACCLAIM

The hand from the cloud extends the gift of patriarchal values and the promise of success in terms of those values if the querent will play by the established rules. The ability to win at traditional games (verbal or computative) is assured. Triumph, power, popularity, fame, conquest, ego-fulfillment—this is the card of the potential leader, champion, hero provided the querent or one near her is willing to perform.

Within the structure of patriarchal values and institutions the querent's ambitions will be realized despite seemingly overwhelming odds. The card may mark the birth of something heroic in the temperament through this touching of the source of social power. The querent may achieve some intellectual excellence or she may experience a personal empowerment, a sense of inner strength which will be externalized in worldly success.

Traditional meaning:

Power and justice which maintain world order. Success, strength, force. All enterprises will succeed. Excessive degree in everything.

Reversed: REFUSAL OF THE GIFT OF POWER (also Power-Tripping)

A rejection of power on the patriarchy's terms out of fear of what it could/would do personally or out of political/ethical reasons. Or perhaps the cost of constant high-voltage performance is too great. Or perhaps the querent refuses to give up her roots, her upbringing, her culture.

Possibly the seeking of power out of ego motives or for ultimately self-destructive reasons. The tendency to be carried away by fame and flattery.

Perhaps a fall from fame or a failure to achieve it when desired. The querent or one close may be being used by "kingmakers" behind the scenes, urged to sell out to the dominant culture where she will have no power but only fame.

Traditional reversed meaning:

Tyranny. Self-destruction. Negative force, uncontrolled violence, wanton destruction.

TWO OF SWORDS

Upright: LACK OF PERCEPTION

The figure is hoodwinked in some way by the patriarchy and pledged to it by her bearing of its arms. She is remarkably balanced for one blindfolded—so balanced in fact that she may not move unless she begins to understand her position. Her back is to the ocean and moon so that even if her eyes were open she would not see the real sources of her strength.

The querent or one near her has accepted the rules, the patterns of law and order, and she refuses (through strong conditioning) to believe she is unhappy or in any way oppressed. She closes off all but her own mind, refusing even to accept sense data close at hand. Perhaps she believes that mental clarity alone without the chaos of emotions is the goal of life. Or, perhaps she is locked into a state of defensiveness which entails blocking out the external world, as well as closing off her own unconscious.

There is something vital that is not being observed. Perception of it would entail movement from the present situation.

Perhaps some threat of physical blindness to the querent or one near.

Traditional meaning:

Balanced force, stalemate. Tension in a relationship. Peace restored, yet tension remaining. Temporary amnesty.

Reversed: DAWNING PERCEPTION

On a psychological level the beginning of consciousness or clicks of recognition. The realization of having been hoodwinked, perhaps for all of one's life. "You have a choice the moment you realize you have not had a choice."

The beginning of movement. The start of some painful change in one's life. Growth. Understanding and perhaps resentment of the blindfold and the swords. Realizing isolation. Beginning to seek "home" with others.

Traditional reversed meaning:

A release from some sort of captivity. Changes, but sometimes in the wrong direction. Betrayal, deceit.

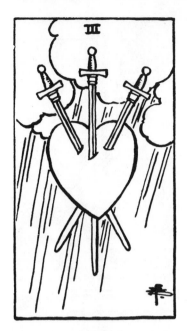

THREE OF SWORDS

Upright: ROMANCE
(also Emotional Intensity)

Romantic love and violence: the patriarchy's perpetual paradox. Genuine love and the *power-over* mindset cannot co-exist. Hence the necessity for the death of love at the hands of duty or honor or patriotism or Christ or law or civilization. The best the patriarchy can do is make such a death noble and rhapsodize about the tragic pain of those involved.

The card demonstrates the social order's attitude toward love: either its excitement fades into mediocrity (is it then still "true love"?), or its exclusive existence (between two only, please) is invaded by a third party, thus necessitating love's tragic death.

The querent or one near her is in love. Exotic highs. Thrills and sheer delight. Sexual attraction. The romantic mode. All the Hollywood accoutrements. Intensification of relationships in the traditional manner. Noble pain and agony.

Also, possible release of suppressed emotion in the face of sterile rationality.

Traditional meaning:

Sorrow, separation, absence (of a loved one). Strife, quarreling with love partners.

Reversed: UNROMANCE
(also Emotional Tedium)

A denial of romance for an attempt to see a relationship more honestly. Less of excitement and adventure and more of the real work on relationships, both interpersonal and in task-oriented situations.

Perhaps a longing for excitement, a missing of intensity that once was a part of one's life; a fear of dullness or boredom that asks the question, "What price honesty?"

A relationship involving the querent falters because sexual desire is subdued or participants feel "dull."

Traditional reversed meaning:

Mental anxieties, loss, upheaval—but in a lesser degree. Great disorder, physical or mental.

FOUR OF SWORDS

Upright: RELIEF FROM DUTIES

Retirement, someone being moved aside, particularly someone who is a threat to the situation or structure. Being put out to pasture, or, in an indirect way, deprived of power. Perhaps incarceration or confinement to a mental institution "for one's own good." Manipulation of someone with unacceptable views into a position where she can no longer do harm.

The querent or someone near her has become a threat on some level. She has thus been kicked upstairs to a less powerful position, or retired, or relieved of duties. Transfer, perhaps, to another area.

A de-powering of the person by subtle and ostensibly supportive means. Release from the pressures of the job within the system.

Possibly a laying to rest of the powers of reason and judgement. A letting go of some long held rational position. A voluntary, perhaps defensive, withdrawal. A yielding to some non-rational function. Thus a connecting card to the suit of cups.

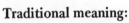

Traditional meaning:

Retreat, exile, solitude, repose. Rest after illness.

Reversed: CIRCUMSPECT ACTIVITY

Guarding one's occupation of a power position either in a job or political situation, perhaps even within an interpersonal situation. Awareness of all aspects of the situation so that attempts made to relieve the querent of her duties does not catch her unawares. Careful control of a situation or activity. Full but circumspect use of the position; political activism within the system.

The querent or one near her plays a careful game. Maintaining a delicate balance.

Holding on to reason in the face of chaos. Judging carefully the circumstances and consequences.

Traditional reversed meaning:

Forced banishment, seclusion. Renewed activity. Social unrest. Circumspection, precaution.

FIVE OF SWORDS

Upright: SEIZING POWER IN THE SYSTEM (also Victory Through Unethical Tactics)

There has been some contest within the system, a debate, a negotiation, even a physical battle, and some members of the patriarchy have been beaten at their own game. One perhaps new to the system has achieved some power within it. The main figure has taken a first step toward power. She has won the swords.

The card may mean the movement into some power slot of a person more dedicated to personal ends than to revolution. An opportunist may have moved up a notch. Some empty victory over another because of the system's hierarchical structure and competitive attitudes.

Querent should be careful not to use unethical tactics, or should be on guard against such tactics being used by others. Danger is in internalizing the values of the system. Water is close at hand suggesting that the figure does stay in touch with some non-dominant (emotional) values.

A protracted struggle—with the self or others—in which the querent realizes that continuation is defeating.

Traditional meaning:

Defeat, degradation, dishonor. Destruction of others. Unfairness. A need to swallow pride and accept the inevitable.

Reversed: DIVIDED AND CONQUERED (also Loss Through Unethical Tactics)

Either interpersonal or political strife within the ranks of those who would be allies. Someone has been bought out or tokenized at the expense of another. Lack of solidarity in the workplace, or one group of persons being set against another. A fighting over the crumbs or minor benefits while top power holders gain even more influence/money.

The querent or one near her may be done in by unethical or unsisterly means, either because of the system's structure or because of her gullibility. A more healthy skepticism is in order.

Women or counter culture groups have somehow been divided and temporarily vanquished.

There may be some loss of verbal or analytic skills, or some defeat in a verbal arena. The need for improving such skills.

Traditional reversed meaning:

Loss or defeat as a result of weakness, pride, indecision, treachery.

SIX OF SWORDS

Upright: RETREAT FROM TRAVAIL

Retreat from temporary failure. Some attempt to change patriarchal structures or individuals has fallen into futility. The figure takes the child (herself) to a place of rest, having paid some boatman too high a price so she can gain quiet.

Drawing back from some venture perhaps to catch one's breath, to retrench, or remake strategy. Political disappointment. A possible trip, taking the querent away from the source of travail.

Reason and justice may have been defeated by mob power or fanaticism. Reason and clarity must retreat.

Responsibility for someone or some enterprise weaker than the querent. Or the querent is herself the ferry person, serving as some means of transport (a facilitator, an ear, a temporary means of escape) for another or others.

Traditional meaning:

Success after anxiety. A journey away from trouble. Troubles not completely over, but some obstacle has been removed allowing further progress.

Reversed: ENDURANCE

No defeat, but no victory either. A stasis. The status quo prevails. There is no change in the challenges to the patriarchy. Business as usual.

No growth or dialogue. Some situation badly needing clarity or mediation is suspended in bad feelings. A stand-off. No one is moving.

Perhaps loss of zeal, or loss of possibility for present action. Endurance is the only recourse. Hang in.

Traditional reversed meaning:

A need for continuing struggle. Further obstacles will be encountered. No immediate way out of present difficulties.

SEVEN OF SWORDS

Upright: RIP OFF
(also Stealing the Weapons of the Enemy)

The harlequin-like figure (thief, knave, hustler) has successfully stolen some weapons—but not all—from the patriarchy's battle camp (a xerox machine?) and is appropriating them for herself and others of like mind. Under the very eyes of the enemy she has tiptoed from the tents with the useful items.

Deception. Fraud and roguery in service of the revolution. Cleverness. Stealth. Creative undermining. Executed, however, in a very individualistic way without support from others and, hence, dangerous. The querent or one near her is successful in such deception, or may be called on to use such tactics.

Or, possible sense of betrayal on querent's part. Someone she trusted worked against her, ripping off her ideas, resources, or emotions.

Also, can be a warning against direct confrontation when facing a powerful enemy (e.g. the patriarchy).

Traditional meaning:

New schemes, design, attempt. Unstable effort. A card that suggests caution and vigilance.

Reversed: NARROW ESCAPE
(also Caught In The Act)

Failure to complete the plan; apprehension by authorities or narrow escape from detection. Some misplaced trust, perhaps.

Some failure to perform without detection. An inability to lie or to deceive in interpersonal or in political matters. The querent or one near her has "too honest a face" or cannot bring herself, even as a strategy, to dissemble. Her fear of being caught itself becomes the danger. Or she has too much invested in it to be able to betray the system.

The querent must beware of attempting theft without support or planning. A risk, perhaps, that burns and thus ensures learning from the experience.

Or perhaps one who could have betrayed the querent remained loyal after all.

Traditional reversed meaning:

Good advice, instruction. Surrender when vicory is almost within grasp. Possibility of a windfall.

EIGHT OF SWORDS

Upright: IMPRISONMENT

The card most literally addressing the matter of violence against women. The querent or one near her must deal with rape, pornography, or some physical abuse of herself or other women.

The bound woman is abandoned to the rising tide for crimes against some established order—not being a proper woman; a lesbian, a witch. Punishment is either the direct consequence of her actions, or simply a way of making her an example.

It is significant that she is alone, isolated from others. Since she is blindfolded she may not know her fate. She waits almost passively, perhaps still trusting some unworthy agent. The swords, if she but explored their presence, could cut her bonds and give her freedom.

Perhaps a refusal to use patriarchal methods (to cut with the swords). Perhaps even a refusal to reason, to verbalize, or to assess a situation analytically. Bondage and danger resulting from a conservative, even purist, attitude. Or perhaps a principled pacifist who rejects the weapons of violence even when they could save her.

Querent could also be feeling trapped, immobilized, bound by a situation in which she feels lost or out of control. Thus a card related to The Devil.

Traditional meaning:

Shortened force. Energy wasteage through indecision. Restriction or imprisonment through indecision.

Reversed: REPRIEVE

Resistance to condemnation, fighting against it. Freedom from imprisonment. Escape from passivity and death by ingenuity and determination.

Some individual action taken against the institutions that physically abuse women.

The drive to self-preservation combines with cool-headedness to allow the querent or one associated to sidestep a perilous situation. A desperate embrace of patriarchal methods, perhaps even violence, for one's own survival.

Perhaps some power-that-is has her released at the last moment or she is rescued by friends.

Traditional reversed meaning:

Release from restriction, from fear.

NINE OF SWORDS

Upright: FEAR

The woman awakes in despair from nightmares, perhaps an increasingly common occurrence. She is horrified at— and hides her eyes from—the realization of the dangers of her life: the consequences of her current involvements, her powerlessness, her commitments, her overextension, her allegiance to an exploitative system. Threats of death, judgement, or pain hang over her head. There is no rest from the dangers, not even in dreams.

Perhaps the death, failure, or depowering of someone close or significant. Perhaps guilt.

Some disruption in the querent's life because of the constant or sudden realization of menace. Someone or some agency is opposed to her or seeking her out with malice. There is an invasion of her dreams; fears of insanity. Hallucination, perhaps, or seeming distortions of reality out of heavy pressures or fears.

Traditional meaning:

Suffering, oppression, illness, pain. Utter desolation and despair. Death of someone close to the querent. A card of bad omen.

Reversed: DEMOLISHING FEAR
(also Overcoming Despair)

Opening one's eyes to face danger, perhaps to claim it. Feeling the fear, yielding to it. Patient analysis or slow deliberate action to remove each individual sword. Careful dealing with each threat without causing harm. Slow recovery from near madness.

The querent or one near her needs to deal with each menace by herself. Not a shared action, though others may be supportive. The need to exercise clarity and determination in a patient and plodding way in order to remove threats to survival.

Perhaps some realization that excessive analytic activity needs grounding in physical work or emotional release.

Traditional reversed meaning:

Patience will cure hurts and loss. Strength and new life won through suffering.

TEN OF SWORDS

Upright: ENDS JUSTIFY
(also Ruin)

There has been a ritual killing and a body has been left without burial rites. A big thing has been made of the killing as if the person were some symbol—a sacrifice or maybe a scapegoat—offered up *by* the patriarchy or *to* it in place of others.

The querent or someone close to her may be sacrificed without her consent; or she may be called on to sacrifice some part of herself "for the sake of the cause" or for "good cause." "The end justifies the means" is the rationale undergirding this card.

Also, some suggestion of logic or the discursive mode as a killer: "Analysis presupposes a corpse," or, to break down or tear apart requires the death of something non-rational. The querent or one near her refuses to recognize the dangers of repressing the creative for the sake of the analytic. Or the card could also signify the end of a delusion, release from some obsession.

The querent may need to deal with death.

Traditional meaning:

Ruin, desolation, disruption of one's life. Trouble notwithstanding material security. This card represents the bottom of the cycle of misfortune, things can only improve. Not a card of violent death.

Reversed: NONVIOLENCE
(also Recovery)

Refusal to justify violence as a means to some desired end. Violent acts make violent people, and even failure is better.

The querent or one near her refuses to participate in violent action even though that action seems to be for her own or other women's safety. She thereby loses peer group support, political clout, or interpersonal power.

Perhaps wholistic and non-rational avenues of discrimination are tapped and energies are released to balance the threat of fragmented rationality or tunnel vision.

Traditional reversed meaning:

Courage to pick up the pieces. Temporary improvement. An apparent lifting or problems, but suffering will continue.

PAGE of SWORDS.

PRINCESS OF SWORDS
(Or Page)

Upright: PATRIARCHAL YOUTH

A young person practices wielding the power of the dominant culture. Training in control.

This figure pursues the American Dream. She may be an ardent Christian, A Rainbow Girl, a Mason, DAR member, Girl's State Governor, finding self-expression always within the confines of the value system she has been trained within. The distinct impression of this young person is that she will not change substantially; life seems too satisfying to want an alteration of the system.

She could also be the co-opted feminist—the a-bigger-piece-of-the-pie-for-me feminist. She is in danger of alienating herself from others and from her own feelings.

She is somehow associated with the querent or is alive within the querent.

Either a young woman who sees motherhood as a woman's only career and who still identifies with the system's values, or a young man being molded by the system. Could also be the male-identified revolutionary woman—fighting for the revolution that sees women's rights as appropriate "later."

Traditional meaning:

A vigilant, subtle, active person with an active intelligence. A person adept at uncovering the unknown (spying for the police?). Skilled in the use of diplomacy, perhaps in government service. An expert negotiator on behalf of her superiors. A card signifying vigilance. Perhaps the card of the informer, the infiltrator.

Reversed: COUNTER-CULTURE YOUTH

A revolutionary young person, a counter-culture youth who in ideology and lifestyle seeks transformation of the present system. The nonconformist who challenges the querent or who is part of the querent, expressed or unexpressed.

Openness to change, rebellion. Often hotheaded action out of anger. Sometimes too "laid back" to resist oppression.

There is danger that in rebelling against patriarchy some helpful skills may also be discarded: clear-thinking, keen discrimination in reason, assertiveness.

Traditional reversed meaning:

A person who is an imposter. Someone who looks for hidden weaknesses in people while overtly giving friendship. The qualities of deviousness, hypocrisy, cunning, indiscretion. A card of deceit.

PRINCE OF SWORDS
(Or Knight)

Upright: HASTY REVENGE
(also Thoughtless Action)

KNIGHT of SWORDS.

The established order responds in a hasty and violent way to some action on the part of the people or someone disempowered. May be in heavy police or military action repressing minority elements. An unnecessary rash display of strength, paranoia, vengeance. (Kent State, massacre of the SLA.)

A close relative of the braggart soldier, rattling swords and making bold threats. The hasty action may actually be against her/his better judgment, but necessary in order to fulfill her/his boasts.

The querent may herself be the knight responding hastily to some enraging circumstance—not necessarily political. The danger is great that she may behave in this way since women and other nondominant groups have not until recently been able to emulate white knights dashing across open country on missions of grave import. She is likely to jump too quickly to avenge another, or to protect what is dealt to her. Thoughtless action, no matter what the motivation, has dangerous consequences.

Traditional meaning:

Tyranny over the weaker. A person always ready to start a fight. Prone to look to violence for solutions. Fierce in action, but little staying power.

Reversed: CALCULATED TYRANNY

Cool and calculated retaliation. Quiet power. Patient insidious moves. Either the patriarchy or the querent schemes carefully over an extended period of time in order to "set right" some "insubordinate" action. Possible someone closely associated with the querent is capable of such action.

The justification for the action may be that it is for the victim's own good. Some move to convert rather than to conquer outright. Colonization as opposed to military invasion.

Traditional reversed meaning:

Heroic action, martial bravery. The archetypical warrior. The coming or going of misfortune. A card of vengeance through action.

KING ♂ SWORDS.

KING OF SWORDS
Upright: PATRIARCHAL MAN

The conservative man, supporter of law and order, control, and retribution. No respecter of differences, he is probably white supremacist, Christian moralist, homophobic, misogynist—and would deny only the latter. Not necessarily a wealthy financier or otherwise powerful man, but a true believer in the superiority of patriarchal values. He may well be in the police or legal profession, dispensing justice, or in the legislature making righteous laws.

On an intellectual level, the hyper-rationalist who dismisses all phenomena which cannot be scientifically validated—in the manner of Bishop Berkeley who said, "in the dark if I can't see you, you can't be you."

The card suggests a person in the querent's life; but the patriarchal characteristics may be a part of the querent herself—she may be overly rigid or judgmental.

Traditional meaning:

This card is the minor arcana equivalent of The Emperor. It stands for the law of the dominant patriarchal order. Power, strength, superiority, authority. An experienced, controlled, commanding man of highly analytical intelligence. The advocate of modernity at the expense of tradition.

Reversed: PATRIARCHAL DEFECTOR

Changing man. The older man whose life in support of the system changes radically as a result of his consciousness. He is moving from restrictive thinking to tolerance. The liberal man, he may still be dangerous at base, and one who may need thanks and affirmation for every politically correct behavior.

Perhaps radical changes within the querent if her attitude and position in the system have been similar to the patriarchal man. She attempts to confront racism within white women, and class issues on the part of women of privileged background; a "seeing anew" of unconscious ideologies like ageism, able-bodied chauvinism, heterosexism, human chauvinism, as well as race and class bias. The reversed king can thus be a bridge card to the suit of cups.

Traditional reversed meaning:

Selfishness and cruelty bordering on sadism. A dangerous man who may cause chaos in the name of order.

QUEEN OF SWORDS

Upright: PATRIARCHAL WOMAN

The patriarchy's woman, perhaps even ruling class. One who believes in individual power and the virtues of patriarchal tools. Perhaps an academic woman whose mastering of male models and process threatens to cut her off from other parts of herself.

The male-identified woman who has made it in the system or who is the perfect housewife/mother/grandmother. She supports the system with as much vigor as any man, has never felt oppressed and believes women's liberation is an excuse for shrill, pushy women to complain instead of picking themselves up by their bootstraps and making something of themselves.

"Her face is chastened through suffering"—perhaps through repressed anger, and through the conviction that "you have to be tough to survive." She may have a man's job, and may despise women—herself included—although, paradoxically, she could be a closet lesbian.

Somehow she touches the querent's life or is a part of the querent's self. She is dangerous.

Traditional meaning:

A woman who suffered loss and privation. Quick-witted, perceptive, and subtle. May signify mourning, absence.

Reversed: LATE REVOLUTIONARY BLOOMER

The older woman who changes her life after years of supporting the system. The radical turn of events that transforms a value system or all behavior patterns is the more striking because of her age.

A woman integrating herself, touching emotional and intellectual reality, psychic and material worlds. Changing woman.

Somehow she touches the querent's life or is a part of the querent's self, particularly as the querent examines the subtleties of her own oppressiveness—of class, race, able-bodiedness, sexual orientation, age, human arrogance. The reversed card is thus a bridge card to the suit of cups.

Traditional reversed meaning:

A narrow-minded, deceitful and malicious woman. Unreliable, but with a good exterior.

The Cups

THE SUIT OF CUPS

(Water, intuition, the unconscious, feeling and emotion. The suit of the self.)

This suit speaks of the relationship to the self, to the parts of the self and to others in interpersonal contacts. It is the area of psychological growth, of the internal quest for integrity. That integrity, bound up as it is with feminist values, rejects the exploitation of any physical difference (race, sex, or bodily ability). It affirms those qualities of traditionally secondary importance—qualities associated with women and, by extension, other nondominant groups: emotionality, the unconscious, the occult, intuition, bodiness. Hence the suit is associated with the priestess. It calls for an integration of these qualities with the more traditionally acceptable characteristics (masculine, white, able-bodied): mind, consciousness, energy and strength.

The journey suggested by the cups is to authentic relationships where whole persons interact with as few power games as possible. It is a journey away from the half-persons who have to depend on each other for personal fulfillment (as in the heterosexual model that all of us are still slave to on some level or in some degree).

Cups are vessels of individual feelings, of psychic energy, of intuitive or unconscious material, particularly as women seek their own identity and happiness. It suggests the necessity to intrapersonal confrontation with deeply-embedded attitudes and the struggle that persists between whatever is "natural" and that which is "conditioned" in the female psyche. It is the suit of self-knowing.

Like the suit of pentacles, cups have to do with *perception* and *understanding* more than with *judgements* and *actions* (the functions of swords and wands). The cups suggest ways of perceiving psychic and psychological realities; they open ways for the understanding of such realities without the necessity of evaluations or judgements.

ACE ♦ CUPS.

ACE OF CUPS

Upright: THE GIFT OF THE SELF

The promise of self-fulfillment. The extended hand holds the cup that runs over back into the waters of the unconscious and intuitive knowledge. The offering to oneself of her emotionality and sensuality (the five streams) and of her own pleasure in creativity and self-expression.

The offering to women of what already belongs to them but which is frequently unclaimed. The vision of the individuated self, there for the taking, and the suggestion of collective potential as well—the return of the individuated streams or drops of water to the larger body. The stirrings of social consciousness through interpersonal relations.

Beauty, pleasure, self-love relationship. The vision of what with work the querent could achieve. The dream of homecoming to the self. Overflowing with good feelings.

For the querent a promise of creativity and inspiration which will result from openness to and close rapport with the subconscious mind.

Traditional meaning:

Fulfillment, fullness, abundance, happiness, contentment. Productivity, inspiration, creativity. A very good card.

Reversed: REFUSAL OF SELF

Some withholding of the gift of the self or some obstacle to it. Perhaps a cut-off of the stream of emotionality or intuitive perception; a blockage of the unconscious. Perhaps extreme outward orientation in flight from the self. Denial of growth.

The querent or one near her struggles with (and perhaps denies) messages from her internal self. She will not change until she is ready; when she is ready nothing will stop her from changing. She may distance only temporarily from self-knowledge or from deep relationships.

As a flight from self-love the card reversed suggests flight from womanlove, lesbian love.

Traditional reversed meaning:

Unrequited love, false love. Sterility. Instability.

TWO OF CUPS

Upright: INTERPERSONAL GROWTH

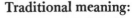

The vow to harmonize and balance in oneself the societally-defined "feminine" and "masculine" elements. Not yet a union of these elements, but the recognition of their existence as the foundation of all power dynamics; a suggestion of hope that they might be reunited.

Often the vows of affection with a loved one. And the corollary: that projections laid upon each other will be called home, that the relationship will grow to the extent that unbalanced qualities and power dynamics are named, struggled with and dissipated.

The querent or one near her is committed to or is about to be committed to exploring personal habits of manipulation or defensiveness particularly as these habits affect friends, lovers. Perhaps the interpersonal struggle of a racially mixed couple or of two persons of different class backgrounds, different physical capabilities, different sexual orientations.

This card can also represent the feminist woman who struggles to achieve a non-repressive and non-oppressive relationship with a man; or it could simply signify a profoundly committed love between two people.

Traditional meaning:

Harmony of the male and female principles. Co-operation, mutual understanding. Love, affection, friendship.

Reversed: INTERPERSONAL STALEMATE

Painful battles within the self without resolution, usually because the person fails to recognize some power dynamic. Lack of internal balance between "feminine" and "masculine" qualities.

Painful battles with others, usually in the romantic mode, where resolution seems impossible and quarrels seem destructive.

The querent or one near her may not be able to face elements of her own oppressiveness (her ageism, her racism, etc.,) or she may be unable to make clear her own feelings of being oppressed by a partner. She may be a woman who allows herself to be dominated by another woman or by a man who refuses to struggle for an egalitarian relationship.

Traditional reversed meaning:

Disunity, misunderstanding. Separation, divorce or deceit in an emotional relationship. Lust, cupidity.

THREE OF CUPS

Upright: TOWARD INTERDEPENDENCE

A celebratory atmosphere like the first blush of sisterhood suggested in the Four of Wands. Here, however, the mood has deeper meaning, less frivolity; here are the deeper significance of intimate personal relationships interwoven with more than one other person. There is a toast to struggle together on issues intricately related to each one's personal growth—far more than the traditional one-to-one pledging or the general toasting to all women. A celebration of extended love relations or of a potentially collective union founded on love, including physical love and work. Perhaps a commitment to be a family, to involve children, older women. Just a step away from concerted social or political action.

The querent or one close celebrates a joint venture, conceived in love. Perhaps she specifically denies patriarchal monogamy or moves away from exclusive relationship to wider sharing. There is a conscious bonding with more than one woman, but it is a bonding that is spontaneous and celebratory.

Traditional meaning:

Success, abundance. Favorable beginning of a new venture. Joyous outcome of an undertaking.

Reversed: COLLECTIPHOBIA

Rejection of deep interpersonal relationships with more than one person. Possible fear of lesbian love. Perhaps intense individuation.

The querent or one near her fears intimacy or intimacy of a new kind, i.e., with a group. Or she experiences feeling of having been left out or excluded from some group. Perhaps she realizes that the bonding of some women has led to the exclusion of others. Perhaps withdrawal from "grouping."

The card suggests that there may be serious examination of what it means to choose a person, to "like" someone, to "be attracted to" someone. Attempts to understand the "chemistry" that goes between women.

Traditional reversed meaning:

Pain which results from self-indulgence. Sensual indulgence. Extravagance with negative results.

FOUR OF CUPS

Upright: REFLECTION
(also Re-Evaluation)

An alienated or distanced phase. Deliberate withdrawal and refusal to participate in relations or even in ordinary day-to-day functions. A surfeit of people or disgust and disappointment at failure of communication in relationships. Self-imposed emotional and personal isolation; obliviousness to others. Boredom with the self.

The querent or one close is in a period of re-assessment, stocktaking, searching for new values. She may distrust all that has gone before. She contemplates what may come. An immobilization that comes from a profound sense of discontent with her life.

A deliberate withdrawal from others to process previous input and to clear the circuits. Self-touch or grounding.

Traditional meaning:

Ennui, surfeit, the salt hath lost its savor. Dissatisfaction with existing values. A once passionate relationship loses its flavor.

Reversed: EXTROVERSION

A time of outreach to people, either out of flight from oneself or out of a strong sense of self. There may be no need for contemplation and reflection since the querent or one near her is well-grounded within her own psychological environment. She reaches out authentically.

Or, the querent may be excessively extroverted in a driven way, out of fear of losing others. She may have lost the capacity to retreat for reflection. Or she may have no ability to say "no." An overloading of the circuits and no time allocated for processing input.

Traditional reversed meaning:

Waking from a period of contentment. New interests, new instruction, new relationships instituted after a period of withdrawal.

FIVE OF CUPS

Upright: DESPAIR (also Disillusionment)

A desolate and despairing place in the emotional odyssey. Wrapped in a cloak of mourning the figure contemplates the three overturned cups as the wine (or blood?) seeps into the ground.

Disappointment. Relationship seems impossible—either paired relationships, friendships, or work relations. All seems transient. Broken trust, misunderstanding.

The querent may feel hurt by others or despairing at what seems to be her own capacity to destroy. Self-denigration. Some sense of being controlled by internal destructive forces perhaps too deep to understand. The querent does not dare reach out to the remaining cups in case these may also be lost.

A sense of futility and lack of clarity. The river of the unconscious reminds us that we are in its power and act very seldom out of conscious motives.

The querent focuses on the bleakness of the past, failing to see the things of value that remain in the present.

Traditional meaning:

A sense of loss, yet with a sense that all is not hopeless. Alternatives remain to be explored. Relationship without real love.

Reversed: RISING HOPE

Revival after despair. New hope after disillusionment. Circumstances take on more meaning; relationships seem more creative.

The querent may realize that no one destroys another person in a relationship without some cooperation from the other party. She may gain greater knowledge through this transcending of despair and disappointment. Struggles, both internal and interpersonal, again seem worthwhile.

Traditional reversed meaning:

Hopeful expectation. The return of enjoyment. Return of an old friend or the resumption of relationship with an old lover.

SIX OF CUPS

Upright: CHILDHOOD
(also Strength from the Past)

A journey back to childhood and early home circumstances; memories and fantasies reconstruct significant occasions. A place of early memories which one presently feels a need to visit. A redemption of the child and re-ignition of the spark of play, the spirit of fun.

Some understanding of present behavior through a link to the past. For once the cups are full. The card thus suggests that there is a fullness, a wholeness in childhood that the querent seeks or is discovering.

Perhaps the querent needs to deal with her present relationships to children and with the things that are real to children. The place of children in the querent's life is in question. Or she is somehow responsible for children. A possible extension of the home/family scene is suggested: the relationship to older/ old people and the querent's responsibility to/for some older person, particularly where the older person is dependent on others for physical needs.

Traditional meaning:

A card of the past, looking back, happy memories. Things of the past bringing pleasure in the present.

Reversed: REFUSAL OF CHILDHOOD

Unhappy childhood or home memories. Some bitterness about one's childhood. Perhaps an inability to relate to children in the present.

The querent or one near her may be misplacing her anger, taking it out on children. Or through some unconscious attitude she may be oppressing a child. Perhaps some struggle with the question of male children.

Inability to find the joy of childhood in oneself. Lack of desire to play, to rejoice in simplicity.

The querent may be hung up on what is past and not be able to live in the present. She may long for the return of the protected and carefree state of "golden" childhood.

Traditional reversed meaning:

Living too much in the past. Nostalgia which prevents one from adapting to changing conditions.

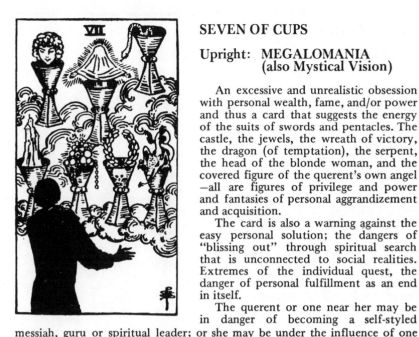

SEVEN OF CUPS

Upright: MEGALOMANIA
(also Mystical Vision)

An excessive and unrealistic obsession with personal wealth, fame, and/or power and thus a card that suggests the energy of the suits of swords and pentacles. The castle, the jewels, the wreath of victory, the dragon (of temptation), the serpent, the head of the blonde woman, and the covered figure of the querent's own angel —all are figures of privilege and power and fantasies of personal aggrandizement and acquisition.

The card is also a warning against the easy personal solution; the dangers of "blissing out" through spiritual search that is unconnected to social realities. Extremes of the individual quest, the danger of personal fulfillment as an end in itself.

The querent or one near her may be in danger of becoming a self-styled messiah, guru or spiritual leader; or she may be under the influence of one who suffers from such delusions of grandeur.

More positively, a mystical experience, an inspirational vision seen "in the glass of contemplation." (Waite)

Traditional meaning:

Castles in the air, illusionary success, unfulfilled promises. Another school of thought sees this card as one of choice: the querent is faced with several choices, one of which is much more significant than the others.

Reversed: LETTING GO

Overcoming inflated personal goals. Grounding in the reality of material existence. A hard look at one's talents and liabilities. A release from ego-gratification or whatever drives one to dreams of personal grandeur at the cost to others.

The querent or one near her emerges from some trial with her ego or with the temptation of material goods or spiritual power. A reaffirmation of the individual as a relational being, not as an acquisitive one.

Perhaps a false mystical experience.

Traditional reversed meaning:

Intelligent selection. Good resolutions. Self-deception.

EIGHT OF CUPS

Upright: MOVING ON
(also Rejection of the Present)

A journey that takes us over the river of the unconscious to we know not where. Continuing, though there is risk. Moving forward into the self in spite of full cups in the external world.

The querent or someone close turns away from individualistic visions and seeks authenticity. She goes deeper, confronting more fears, dropping more defenses, becoming more vulnerable. Still alone, still disillusioned, she is at that point in the journey to the self where she knows the process to be irrevocable. There is no place to go but on; there is no one to accompany us but the moon.

The querent may be breaking with ideas, values or relationships which have outlived their relevance. She journeys to a different and deeper place.

The card may indicate leavetakings—from relationships, values, interests, lifestyles.

Traditional meaning:

Things abandoned as soon as achieved. Misery without cause. Desire to transcend material success. The decline of a matter which the querent had thought to be more important than it really is.

Reversed: GIVING UP
(also Mired in the Present)

A yielding to despair. Self-destructive acts. Perhaps a turn to superficial pleasures and occupation of the senses in a flight from the self. Alcoholism or excessive indulgence in some similar drug is suggested.

Sheer survival may be in question; external conditions are extreme; one crisis after another; the querent or one near her may be exhausted, may not wish to carry on, may feel unable to cope, may find no real sustenance in herself. The card reversed may be a cry for help. The querent or one near yields to the existing conditions of her life even though she senses a need for progression and change.

An unwillingness to risk or a fatigue that prevents risking.

Traditional reversed meaning:

Spiritual development traded for material security. Interest in success. Not willing to risk present gains.

NINE OF CUPS

Upright: SELF-SATISFACTION (also Contentment)

A fulfillment of wishes, desires. Physical and psychological well-being.

The smiling figure sits before nine cups, filled not with material goods but with something intangible, like energy. She seems well-filled with the contents; she may be hosting some celebration to come.

The querent or one near her feels a strong sense of her own integrity. The danger is that she feels "right" (or politically correct) without acknowledging that she may again be confused or in pain or that another may be "right" as well. Her smugness may limit her.

The querent is at the point of conscious self-love; a potential relationship that is free of games seems possible now. Inner security.

Traditional meaning:

Circumstances which facilitate satisfaction, well-being, contentment. Success in everything: relationships, work, creativity. Eden Gray sees this as the wish card, i.e., the querent will get her wish if it turns up in the spread.

Reversed: NEGATIVE SELF-CRITICISM

Disappointment. A wish not yet fulfilled, perhaps because it is desired too intensely, expected with too much fervor. A delay in the assurance of self-love.

Possibility of ill health. Apologies, self put-downs, negative self-criticism. The querent may have a downer experience in the outside world that results in extreme self-hating behavior. Perhaps a call to look at the reasons for such a lapse into negative self-criticism in such extremes.

The querent may lose her sense of self-worth in a quick change of fortune. A plunge into dissatisfaction after riding high.

Traditional reversed meaning:

Illness, material deprivation. Complacency, taking the good things for granted.

TEN OF CUPS

Upright: INTERNAL UNION

Realization of the union of the "feminine" and "masculine" principles sought in the Two of Cups, and the redemption of childhood as well as one's personal history.

The querent's relations with children have reached a new high; relations with old people (with other old people?) may have done the same. She hails the river of unconsciousness from which discoveries will continue to come. There is a recognition of the house—the self—in which the querent will live, a sense of at last being "at home."

A plateau of growth for the querent. Some conflict is resolved, some tension released, some answer discovered. Differences seem to enrich rather than to cause conflict. Interpersonal relations feel solid, ready to grow into new commitments.

The card suggests that social or political action is possible only when self-awareness and personal integration are achieved.

Traditional meaning:

Happy family life. Great friendship. Lasting happiness in an enduring relationship.

Reversed: CRITICISM OF THE PERSONAL

The political stance that expresses disgust with personal search, disdain for individualistic solutions. Suspicions or convictions in the querent that to spend time on herself is a non-political pastime prompted by bourgeois motives. Questioning of the value of the personal quest.

Perhaps the querent or one near is cynical about the propaganda surrounding "sisterhood." Resentment at being duped into even temporary belief in sisterhood's reality. A put-down perhaps with good reason, of personal and interpersonal concerns.

Or the querent may experience irritation and impatience from someone else who disdains the psychological jargon ("internal union," "integration within the self").

Traditional reversed meaning:

Loss of friendship. Selfish exploitation of the goodwill of others.

PAGE of CUPS.

PRINCESS OF CUPS
(Or Page)

Upright: DISCOVERY
(also Imagination)

The fish, inhabitant of the ocean, arises from the depths of the unconscious to where it can be examined, understood. (Waite describes the fish as "pictures of the mind taking form.")

There is some success in work with the unknown, with the unconscious. Some food for thought, for self-examination. The emergence of the intuitive and emotional powers within the querent or the appearance of a person who may help with such discoveries.

The figure communicates with the fish, seeming to listen, to hear some new message. Thus the card suggests the sharing of some secret, or the sharing of some secret about the querent with another person.

The querent might benefit from a slowing down of external activities in order to hear (perceive) intrapersonal messages.

Traditional meaning:

A quiet, imaginative person of artistic bent. Imagination, reflection, mediation.

Reversed: PUZZLEMENT
(also Blockage)

Something puzzling from a nonrational source intrudes upon the querent; a conundrum with no answer. Frustration at a vague sense of unease or near-discovery; at the failure to know and understand.

Perhaps the querent tries too hard to force a message from herself or her surroundings. Or she may be unusually skeptical about the existence of psychic messages. Or she has no time to be open to psychic messages.

Perhaps the destructive use of secret information; perhaps blackmail.

Traditional reversed meaning:

Dilettantism. Vulnerability to seduction. An unpleasant message.

PRINCE OF CUPS
(Or Knight)

Upright: THE NEW WEAPON
(also Search for Intuitive
Knowledge)

KNIGHT of CUPS.

A military messenger. The querent emerges from perceptions of herself and personal struggles into a world of social action, even of battle. The card thus serves as a bridge to the suit of wands, perhaps even the suit of swords.

It suggests a new way to go forth to battle: in an unwarlike fashion. The "weapon" is a cup, a receptacle, as if to suggest that victory lies in being filled, in baptizing, or in giving drink. The gift of imagination, intuition, emotionality, seems held out not so much to the querent as to the world at large—to the patriarchy, perhaps given by the querent.

The Knight is protected but except for the cup is unarmed. The wings suggest she is a bearer of information, of self-knowledge—perhaps that is the alternative to patriarchal alienation. Danger lies in the fact that she rides alone, is contemplating some military action without support.

The card also signifies the querent's determination to fill and to keep filling her cup at the stream of the unconscious.

Traditional meaning:

The bringer of ideas, gifts, opportunities. Arrival, invitation, propositions.

Reversed: PASSIVITY

Failure in the use of the "new weapon" perhaps because of lack of understanding of its strength or because of the querent's repression of her emotional/intuitive side or because the querent has misjudged the recipients of her gift.

Weakness, passivity, inability to withstand the behavior of the enemy. Defeat or disappointment in bringing the message of self-discovery or self-love to others. A premature gift, perhaps.

Traditional reversed meaning:

Duplicity, fraud, trickery. Propositions should be scrutinized with caution.

KING of CUPS.

KING OF CUPS

Upright: FATHER

One of the few clearly male figures in a suit expressive of emotionality and self-awareness; it thus suggests the presence of a man or men who could embody those qualities.

More directly in the journey to the self this card represents the querent's father or strong male adult in her life. The man within the querent's history and within herself who functions as protector, provider, intellect and judge. He is whatever the querent's father has been or is.

A clear indication that feelings about the father must be examined or that "fatherly" qualities must be named, confronted and explored within the self.

Traditional meaning:

A man of ideas, liberal, considerate, idealistic. Willingness to accept responsibility. Power achieved through the use of the mind, creative intelligence.

Reversed: REFUSAL OF THE FATHER

Rejection of the father or of the internal qualities associated with father. The negative father trip.

The querent may question the usefulness of fathering altogether. She may wonder if her own fatherlike characteristics come from nature or from conditioning.

The need to deal with some negativity of relationship with one's real father, either in the present or some aspect of the relationship in the past.

Traditional reversed meaning:

A violent man underneath a calm exterior. Ruthlessness, irresponsibility. Hypocrisy, dishonesty.

QUEEN OF CUPS

Upright: MOTHER
(also Nurturant Intelligence)

In the journey to self this card represents the querent's mother or some other strong female adult in her life. She is whatever the querent's mother has been and/or is. The qualities attributed to her are nurturance, devotion, loyalty, emotionality, intuition, physical endurance.

The card heads the suit of self-knowledge. It suggests that the capacity for growth is passed from mother to daughter, female to female.

Perhaps the nurturance of the self, the discovery and confrontation and affirmation of the internal mother. Also may suggest the querent's own love of children or motherliness toward those who seem as children to her, or toward those she can make into children. The querent may need to become a biological mother.

The querent or one near her is generous in teaching her knowledge, sharing her insights and ideas with others.

Traditional meaning:

A good wife and mother. A woman with the gift of vision. *She sees, but she also acts.* An intuitive woman whose instincts can be trusted.

Reversed: REFUSAL OF THE MOTHER

Denial of the mother; rejection of those qualities associated with mother. The need to slay some extreme motherliness within the self. There is some sense of the mother's betrayal or denial of the querent.

Necessity to deal with some negativity of relationship with the mother in the real world, whether in the present or out of some past circumstance.

Selfish hoarding of knowledge out of fear that others will steal one's insights and overtake one. The querent's growth (intellectual as well as psychological) is stymied by some unwillingness to share or to foster growth in another.

Traditional reversed meaning:

Intelligent, but equivocal and unreliable. A dreamer who cannot be trusted.

The Wands

THE SUIT OF WANDS

(Fire, energy, growth, creativity, the production of ideas. The suit of those who struggle together.)

The feminist movement is made up of women seeking a change in the world's social order. It is composed of women seeking new energy and new uses of all energy, new life for a ravaged planet. It is further comprised of an infinite variety of women whose differences in history, outlook and style produce conflict. The wands are the suit of sisterhood and they represent struggles within that sisterhood over all the deep issues of our time: race, class, affectional preference, age, physical ability, and of course sex. On overt or hidden levels the wands address such issues as: leadership, ethical use of energy, empowerment, competition, collectivity, motherhood, criticism, sexuality, and gender identification.

Wands are always in leaf, that is, growing and energy filled. They are also potential weapons, digging sticks, walking aids, magic rods, instruments of protection, and a building material which can be used to construct bridges, houses, and rafts. They may bring us messages—hunches, judgements or discernments that we can act upon. As witching sticks they can aid us in deciding the nature of some unseen element in the immediate environment.

Wands suggest the connection with the earth and the regeneration of life, both animal and plant kingdoms. Lions (cats, the companions of witches in life and in death) are synonymous with wands in the Apocalypse. Fire or energy is the suit's recognizable characteristic.

Like swords, the wands are a suit of *judgement* and *action* rather than *perception* and *understanding* (the function of pentacles and cups). Unlike the suit of swords the suit of wands suggests judgement on the basis of the non-rational: hunches or "vibes" rather than reasons; the actions suggested by the wands on the basis of such judgements or discriminations tend to be rebellious and revolutionary, not supportive of the status quo.

ACE of WANDS.

ACE OF WANDS

**Upright: THE GIFT OF
WOMANLOVE
(also Innovation)**

The gift suggests profound social change through the action of women. The promise of fulfillment. The suggestion is of something very ancient and very common which is also a brand new thing in the world: a social phenomenon built on female values and revering all women. A global rising up of women to redeem the earth.

An enterprise is begun. The dawn of some collective action. The second wave of feminism enacted world-wide out of women's pain.

There are green sprouts on the wand; other green leaves fall like the fiery yods (see The Tower and The Moon). The river of the unconscious flows toward purple-white mountains. A building or a town tops the hill. A natural landscape—rural, of the people, of laborers, working women.

The card of primal energy, it suggests foundations/beginnings/initiatives. A surge of personal growth and development.

Traditional meaning:

The start of something new. The beginning of a journey, an adventure.

Reversed: REFUSAL OF WOMANLOVE
(also Postponement)

Comfort with present circumstances or belief in the patriarchal system. Some inability or lack of desire on the querent's part to move toward other women, either because of her racism/physicalism/homophobia or conversely because other women have for so long been her enemies or oppressors.

False starts or immobility. Mistrust of oneself as a woman.

Delay in some political action with other women. Avoidance of some task shared with other women.

The querent or one near may be put off by the romanticization of feminism wherein all women support and love each other, bonding together for the great utopian future.

Traditional reversed meaning:

Cancellation, postponement of a new enterprise. Barrenness.

TWO OF WANDS

Upright: THE POWER OF INTELLECT (also Professional Success)

A privileged woman with the power that position and expertise bestow upon her. The cold patriarchal mountains are not far away but neither is the water of emotionality. Both roses of desire and lilies of pure thought are common decoration in her home. She has the courage and confidence which come from learning and achieved status.

The card has potential for integrating the wands of women with the world but all depends upon how the figure uses her power.

If the querent is a white woman she can rarely hope to be trusted by women of less privilege than she. Her task is to prove her loyalty to other women, with no expectation of recognition or thanks.

The influence of this person is both economic and intellectual. The querent or one near is (or could become) a professional, a woman who has mastered any set of skills valuable to the patriarchy. She thus has some power in that world. A card indicating a desire or need of the querent to control her environment—either for good or bad, depending on her values. A need for mastery, especially self-mastery. A bridge card to the suit of swords.

Traditional meaning:

Fulfillment of purpose. Courage in starting an enterprise pays off in achievement. Maturity. Dominion, rulership.

Reversed: HOSTILITY TO KNOWLEDGE (also Emptiness of Success)

A denial of or a casting aside of the privileges of intellect, knowledge or some patriarchal skill. A refusal to use such privilege as tools. Often the vacillation between hating knowledge for what its holders have done with it and desiring access to knowledge as a basic right.

Some obstacle created by a person with intellectual or professional skills; some use of knowledge against the interests of women (as in health professions, the sciences, law).

The querent may experience some intellectual lack or inability to achieve a skill. Failure to learn. Perhaps fear of such failure. Or perhaps a hostility to the tyranny of the intellect as the only avenue to knowledge.

Traditional reversed meaning:

"The sadness of Alexander amongst the grandeur of this world's wealth." (Waite) A good beginning sours. Success which brings a feeling of emptiness. Achieving a goal which turns out to be worthless.

THREE OF WANDS

Upright: TRADE AND COMMUNICATION

The figure stands further away from the mountains of knowledge than does the figure in the Two of Wands, but her power is plain. Like the intellectual woman she is in danger of forgetting the majority of women in the world as she exploits both people and the earth in her trade. Yet she might call herself a feminist. She stands between two wands—symbolic of life—and her hand is on a third; she is in touch with another more authentic form of being than the one she presently operates within. She is a merchant of some kind, dealing in the transportation of goods and services. Her ingenuity has given her the respect of her associates. Alone she watches her ships setting out for distant lands, travels there herself to "take care of business." A connecting card to the suit of penttacles.

The querent may be a person interested in communication and human relations and the commerce between people. She may also be someone skilled at seeing the connections in life, or someone who seeks to develop and understand connections: where she is, where she has been, where she is going.

Traditional meaning:

The card of the inventor who turns a dream into a reality. Realization of the enterprise (such as that launched in the Two of Wands). Success in a mercantile venture.

Reversed: OBSTACLES TO COMMUNICATION

Ill luck or obstacles from outside in commercial or communication ventures. The opposition comes from a person who has the kind of power described above, or from institutions with such power.

Some enterprise cannot get started due to lack of communication or foul-ups in logistics—getting from one place to another, getting people together for meetings, difficulties with places and times. Or some enterprise among women fails because of the hassles brought by lack of smooth communications.

Possible betrayal of some feminist enterprise by a woman or women who had the power to aid it.

The querent or one near her must deal with difficulties in the exchange of goods or ideas, or with matters of trust among women.

Traditional reversed meaning:

Grandiose schemes which fail. Difficulty in articulating ideas in practical terms.

FOUR OF WANDS

Upright: DELIGHT AND FRIVOLITY
(also Celebration)

Here is the first burst of sisterhood, the rosy glow of women's discovery of other women. Celebration with dance and song, with garlands and games, food and drink.

Harmony and contentment. Perhaps the solidification of a relationship. Sustaining the intensity of such highs is impossible. The glow is bound to fade, and work must begin. But through the struggles we can be sustained by hopes that this celebratory experience will be recaptured in a more authentic and enduring form.

The querent or one near her finds time for joy and play, rest and recuperation; a deliberate temporary turn from political work to the levity of fun and "lesser" concerns.

Also a card suggesting the temporal arts (music, dance, theatre).

Traditional meaning:

Completed harvest, perfected work. Rest after labor. Work that is enjoyed.

Reversed: OVERWORK

Too much seriousness, not enough play. Overemphasis upon political struggles among women. Burnout.

The querent or one near her needs release into some frivolity.

The search for the joys of sisterhood, believed in, but not yet personally discovered. Frustration at the knowledge that other women exist and that they hope for new values, but as yet no personal experience of womanlove.

Possible impatience of long-time feminists with the apparent naivete of women just discovering each other.

Possible conflicts over issues arising at gatherings of women: substance use (alcohol, nicotine, or other drugs), food, children, male children, disabled needs, animals, class and race awareness.

Traditional reversed meaning:

Prosperity and completion, though to a lesser degree than in the card upright.

FIVE OF WANDS

Upright: INTERNAL STRIFE

The wands are used to play a game, perhaps a sort of sporting rivalry—but it's more likely that the card represents genuine strife. The wands are turned against each other instead of being directed outward toward the common enemy. They move in all directions in contrast to the other cards, where they are all directed one way. The sisterhood cannot get it together. Disintegration, at least around certain issues, threatens disruption. Differences may be seen as "better" or "worse." A party line may be emerging and may be being resisted. Issues of group process, personal style, effective strategies, or conflicting values come to an emotional (perhaps physical) climax. Ideological questions surrounding violence against women may become issues between and among women.

The querent is participating in or affected by rumors, gossiping, back-biting, self-aggrandizement, power-tripping, passivity, dishonesty, jealousy, competitiveness, trashing, anger, and pain, escalated by the social system's divide and conquer strategy. At best an open confrontation that testifies to a desire to struggle. Constructive criticism may yet be possible and greater unity may come from the struggle.

Or, the querent is in a state of deep internal conflict—a struggle that can obstruct growth or that can break through problems.

Traditional meaning:

Strenuous competition; conflict which is unavoidable. The prize will have to be fought for. Opposition.

Reversed: TEMPORARY PEACE

Tentative quiet. Possibly genuine harmony with no strife ahead in the immediate future. Things are working well among the persons involved. Important, however, is a sense that strife could arise at any time.

Or, tacit agreement on the part of the group not to confront conflict; suppressed feelings in order to get a job done. Conflict will eventually emerge and demand attention.

The querent may be in the midst of unexpressed hostility; perhaps an explosive situation. Lack of honest struggle; maybe inertia. Avoidance of conflict out of distaste or fear.

Possibly a card of coalitions, working with other groups for mutual goals.

Traditional reversed meaning:

Disputes, litigation. Victory after overcoming obstacles.

SIX OF WANDS

Upright: A LEADER ARISES
(also Victory)

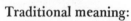

The querent is in a new leadership
position and must deal with all the questions surrounding a single person having
power. The figure has mounted a horse
in order to proceed faster, to sit above
others, to fight from a more advantageous position, or to try out a new perspective. The wreath of victory is on her
head and on her wand. The horse is in
ceremonial rather than battle garb, all
suggesting that the leader has won some
contest. Perhaps the victory is shared
by others—she has just been an out-
standing participant.

The lack of heavy weapons could also
suggest that the victory has been achieved
through the use of skill and diplomacy
rather than the use of power or force.

The horse is traditionally a symbol
of solar energy, suggesting that she leads
in the development of psychic powers or in some understanding of physical/
psychic energy.

Traditional meaning:

Victory after struggle. Success won by hard work. Important news ("such as might
be carried by the King's courier" [Waite]).

Reversed: LEADERLESSNESS
(also Stalemate)

There is some need for a leader. Chaos reigns and nobody is taking responsibility. Nothing is getting done. The tyranny of structurelessness is in
full operation. Either there is no understanding among persons involved of
the power dynamics and the urgency of the situation, or persons capable
of leading hold back out of fear of being authoritarian—or fear of being
trashed.

The querent or one near her may feel a desperate ambivalence: she respects the collective mode but does not want to repress her own abilities.

Relationships may be such that no leader is required. It may be possible
to get tasks done without hassles because there is tacit understanding of each
person's skills and there is a high level of trust. Consensus may be possible.
Near egalitarian relationships could exist.

The card could also suggest tokenism, or the deliberate making visible of
a representative of some minority group for window dressing.

Traditional reversed meaning:

Rewards are slow in coming. Indefinite delay (of news). Fear, as of a victorious
enemy at the gate.

SEVEN OF WANDS

Upright: INDIVIDUAL VERSUS GROUP
(also Taking a Stand)

A single woman is attacked by and is defending herself against other sisters. She stands on some promontory ready to fend them off from above.

"Going against the tide." An assertion of individual needs in opposition to some group. Perhaps a warning against absorption into a false collective identity. The sudden realization of the threat to some part of oneself. Rebellion against being made invisible or feeling insignificant, as in the case of women of color among white women.

Rebellion against the pressure from the group for the individual to accept an internal dominant ideology. The defender may be being attacked because it is thought that she is pushing her own selfish ends to the detriment of the group, or that she is being deliberately disruptive.

The querent may need to stand her ground against the attack of the group. It is important to note that she is on top of the struggle.

Also crystallizes at times as an interpersonal struggle between the needs of the self and the needs (demands) of others.

Traditional meaning:

The querent has the upper hand in a struggle. ("The combatant is on the top and his enemies may not be able to reach him." [Waite]) The querent will obtain victory through sustained effort.

Reversed: INTANGIBLE FEARS

The individual, for some inarticulable reason, fears the group; or, for some inarticulable reason, the group fears the individual.

The querent suffers latent rather than overt insecurity in a group situation. Lack of clarity about motives or about the behavior of members in one's group. Perhaps false fear of group attack. Perhaps an ungrounded suspicion of an individual's selfishness, or a questioning of her motives. Possible suspicion of an individual being an agent, a plant. The feelings are not out in the open. Hostilities must come into the open for the entire group to deal with. An individual may need a champion or supporter in order for conflict to emerge.

Traditional reversed meaning:

Hesitation in the face of opposition brings failure. Caution against indecision.

EIGHT OF WANDS

Upright: PSYCHIC
COMMUNICATION
(also High Velocity
Energy)

Something is flying through the air
over the river of the unconscious. The
positive energy of life is on its way somewhere, perhaps to the querent. The wands
reach through the atmosphere on many
wavelengths to connect women, to become channels of communication.
Something is available that is not being
tapped or used. Some important communication is ready to be expressed from
an unusual source. Forces are moving that
will significantly influence the querent's
life; they may be out of her past, her culture, her family.
The querent may be unconsciously
preparing to make contact with a person
or a group that will be important to her.
A high energy period favorable for
initiating change; or a time of movement and change requiring high energy
expenditure.
A card indicating fast movement, fast growth.
The card of "hunches." The querent should pay special attention to
uninvited images or ideas.

Traditional meaning:

Things get moving after delays. A favorable time for taking trips, for taking the
initiative.

Reversed: BLOCKED ENERGY
(also Wasted Energy)

Earth and water are on top of the energy and entrap it so that it is not
released. Blockage of psychic energy. Lack of communication. Whatever
the message is, it cannot now be received. Bad timing. Energy is dribbled
away too quickly at the start of a matter.
The querent or one near her may be too involved in daily survival to
listen to important messages.
A group of women may be working at odds with another group. Inability
to hear each other. Communication block that prevents important political
action.

Traditional reversed meaning:

Impetuous action which undercuts success. Stagnation, delay.

NINE OF WANDS

Upright: PAUSE IN THE STRUGGLE

The figure has fought and is prepared to fight again. She has been hurt badly enough to require treatment. The issues (the wands) are not menacing—indeed, they seem to back her up. But the internal struggle is exhausting as well as dangerous. She expects to be battered by the patriarchy against whom all the wands fight, but she is only learning to be wounded from within her own ranks. She is reluctant to rejoin the council of wandholders behind her.

May also suggest permanent physical disability or some incapacities of aging. A struggle against stereotypes of disabled people. Querent may risk some disability or be forced to deal with her fear and guilt surrounding physical limitations.

Temporary or permanent dependence upon others. Anger, impotence, guilt on the part of the dependent one; resentment, impatience, flight of one(s) on whom responsibility may fall. A need for understanding and collective action around issues of needs and dependencies.

The querent or one near her needs time for withdrawal to deal with the effects of a deep wound and center the self for further internecine struggles.

Traditional meaning:

Temporary suspension of a struggle. Eventual success after the application of steady force. Strength in reserve. Preparedness.

Reversed: DANGEROUS FATIGUE

Fighting on without rest. Insensitivity to one's own wounds; lack of realization of the damage they do to oneself as well as to others.

The querent suffers battle fatigue and possible lack of perspective induced by that condition. Inefficiency in struggling because of lack of care about herself. Dangerous and unfair behavior as a result of uncared-for injuries— some are perhaps of past origin, e.g., some unfinished business with a group member.

Also, some impatience with persons who raise questions of disability or dependence. Pushing ahead with able-bodied politics while some needs (psychological and physical) are being dangerously ignored

Traditional reversed meaning:

Physical debility, weakness. Obstacles still to be overcome.

TEN OF WANDS

Upright: MARTHA MARTYR

Here is the Martha of the sisterhood: aware that many wands together cannot be broken, yet still believing she must carry them all herself. Inability to let another's task go undone. Backsliding into the old patriarchal principle, "if you want something done, do it yourself." Increasing resentfulness at having to bear the burden alone. Silent or whispered curses at others whose job she is doing because of their lack of responsibility.

The querent has a tendency to bear others' burdens when she has not been asked. She may refuse to let others assume responsibility for themselves. Difficulty in giving up power. The tendency to speak for a group (all black women, all lesbians, all older women) instead of for one's self.

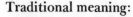

The card also signifies the sense of oppressiveness that can come from trying to handle more than one task at a time. Note that the carrier musters the energy needed to reach the end of the road.

Traditional meaning:

Success which becomes oppressive. Taking on more than can be managed. The burden of too much power.

Reversed: SHARING RESPONSIBILITY

Tempering of the Martha attitude. Dawning of the meaning of collective activity. Struggle within the self and with others in the effort to know when to take action and responsibility and when they belong to others.

An end to mother-hovering. Learning to let others fail. Learning to let go, to delegate responsibility, to see jobs done less than perfectly while others learn.

The querent must resist an enemy that wants to see "leaders" and "spokeswomen." Exercises in group grounding and individual accountability are in order.

Traditional reversed meaning:

Overbearing strength. *The place that the figure is approaching may suffer from the rods that he carries.*

PAGE of WANDS.

PRINCESS OF WANDS
(Or Page)

Upright: VERBAL POWER

This is the spokesperson, the articulate one who has risen from the ranks of laborers and who can speak in the language of the patriarchy itself. She stands on the earth, her wand touching it, joining her to the ranks of women. She remains trusted and trustworthy.

The querent may be an ideologue, who, with her developed skills articulates visions and strategies within the sisterhood. Or she may be one of the sisterhood's spokespersons *to* the patriarch—which would explain her rich dress—the one who can understand and use the written and spoken language that has for so long oppressed women. Perhaps she can write proposals, plead court cases. As a figure committed to negotiating with the patriarchy and to verbal and analytic expression, she makes the card a bridge to the suit of swords.

Traditional meaning:

A person of brilliance and beauty. A messenger with strange news.

Reversed: INARTICULATENESS

Frustration at having important ideas and few skills to articulate them with. Either a temporary or a chronic condition. Or, a sense of loss of verbal or analytic skills after having mastered them. Perhaps a literal loss as with a stroke or physical trauma.

Perhaps words are deliberately held back—out of mistrust of them. A search for some new language instead of the one all women have been taught.

The querent or one near her may struggle with the language as a lately acquired one and feel some question of her legitimacy coming from women who have used the language since childhood.

The oppressiveness of language as a manifestation of a dominant culture.

Traditional reversed meaning:

A superficial untrustworthy person. Misleading information, malicious gossip.

PRINCE OF WANDS
(Or Knight)

Upright: IMPULSIVE ACTION

KNIGHT of WANDS.

The querent or one near her is impatient with words, with intellect, with day-to-day resistance. She longs to take the patriarchy by storm—to arm the troop of women and do battle in the streets. She is full of clever dramatic strategies. She is the adventurer, the gambler, the individualist, the romantic revolutionary more likely to set bombs and hijack planes than to strategize with other women. Spontaneous action on the basis of a hunch is her creed.

Or her action may take the form of a militant separatism, a dismissal of men entirely and a withdrawal with other women from all societal structures. She tends to want utopia immediately and exclusively through magical means.

Her energy, her endurance, her strength, her charisma, all impel women to follow her and sometimes into hasty, regrettable action. Reflective thought is not her strong point. This figure feels constantly restrained by her sisters and often resentful of their plodding.

Traditional meaning:

An attractive, energetic, impulsive person. *The mood of the horse is a key to the character of the rider.* Departure, flight. The coming or going of a matter.

Reversed: INACTION

Indolence, inaction, unwillingness to put out, unwillingness to risk. Much talk, little action. A contentment with the status quo. Lack of revolutionary zeal. Too much fear of danger. Always the reluctant follower.

The querent or one near her is content with having an attitude and seldom initiates action; e.g., she may be non-racist but not anti-racist, non-sexist but not anti-sexist. Or perhaps the querent is disenchanted with the process or strategy of feminists. She may become a drop-out from the movement, deciding against future political commitments. She may simply be burned out and need rest.

For the querent perhaps a time for reflection and self-criticism.

Traditional reversed meaning:

A willfully destructive and cruel person. Indolence, lack of energy.

90

KING of WANDS

KING OF WANDS

Upright: TRUSTWORTHY MAN

This figure is the sympathetic man—a feminist—still powerful, as his robes and demeanor suggest, but yielding significant aspects of his power. The wand is a symbol not of his rule but of a kind of once-removed membership in the ranks of women.

This figure is female-identified, perhaps "sissy"-identified. He understands the auxiliary nature of men in the human species and feels the force and inevitability of the movement to restore the species to its primary (female) foundation. He functions where he can as a buffer against the patriarchy's oppression of women. He is a man of rural origin, and may himself be Native American, black, or of another non-dominant U.S. culture. There is a good chance that he is gay. Certainly he identifies with the cause of held-down people. He is a passionate but careful revolutionary, and one of the useful and important connections between separatist women and the patriarchy. He can be trusted more than other men.

Traditional meaning:

Conscientious, fairminded person. A lover of family life and traditional ways. A good mediator who is able to see all sides.

Reversed: FALSE ALLY

A man who is not to be trusted. A false friend, one who only seems to have committed himself to dealing with his personal sexism or with institutionalized sexism. Perhaps an opportunist who sees a "good thing" in feminism and operates to use the movement for his own gain.

Often the liberal man who seems an ally and whose intentions may seem good, but whose unconscious motives betray him. He is important and powerful because he raises among women deep hopes of reconciliation; yet at the crucial moment is unable to turn over his power or drop the last mask of his masculinity.

In the querent, qualities of prejudice and narrow-mindedness.

Traditional reversed meaning:

An autocratic and cruel person. Intolerance, bigotry.

QUEEN OF WANDS

Upright: ENERGY MENTOR

A black cat sits at her feet while lions play on the tapestry and constitute the arms of her throne. She holds not only the wand, but the sunflower—another natural energy symbol.

She is the mentor of the use of energy in all its forms. The Leo woman; Diana the Huntress, protector of her sisters, avenger of their wrongs; the active and authoritative side of the Empress. She differs from the High Priestess in that she is less an archetype and more a figure of the *future*, or at least more of the *present* than the *past*. She is more active—rather than being symbolic—in her commitment to the politics and practice of womanlove.

The card symbolizes the positive use of power; commitment to women and the non-rational conviction that the power exists only as it is shared among many women.

QUEEN of WANDS.

The querent may discover within herself or in one near her great energy potential, particularly as other women seem to strengthen themselves and one another. There may be question of where to direct the energy, how to use it. Constant questioning about effective strategic action.

The querent may be unexpectedly struck once again by the sometimes awesome power of women.

Traditional meaning:

An active, energetic, generous woman who feels strong ties to nature. An active and practical intelligence.

Reversed: ENERGY MISUSE

Misuse of power or energy, though not through deliberate action. Lack of sufficient knowledge or practice about some aspect of energy.

Perhaps an attempt at individual power rather than collective effort. One vessel cannot carry the energy without danger of freaking, fragmenting, scattering. The querent may have lost the sense of other vessels. She may need "seating" within herself, some focus, some path of action, some meaningful context for action.

Perhaps the need on the part of the sisterhood of a channel, a magician, a person to use energy skillfully and teach about its different forms.

Traditional reversed meaning:

Domineering, obstinate, vengeful (often without reason).

Bibliography

This is by no means a comprehensive bibliography of books on the Tarot. We have selected sources from the large standard literature as well as from the huge recent outpouring of books on the subject.

History of the Tarot:

Paul Huson, *The Devil's Picture Book*, Abacus (London), 1972.

There are several good historical chapters in Huson's book. Alas, his data is not referenced or documented. The book also provides fascinating leads about the history of the symbolism in each of the major arcana. Huson includes an excellent chapter on Tarot spreads.

Stuart Kaplan, *An Encyclopedia of the Tarot*, U.S. Games (New York, 1978.

A large, expensive book, lavishly illustrated, featuring a comprehensive and invaluable description of Tarot packs from the oldest to the most recent. It also contains a valuable bibliography of historical and rare books on the Tarot.

Gertrude Moakley, *The Tarot Cards Painted by Bembo*, New York Public Library (New York), 1966.

A penetrating, scholarly study of the Visconti deck—the earliest, full Tarot deck extant—analysing in particular the meaning of the cards' symbolism in their historical context. A truly fascinating book.

Using and Interpreting the Tarot:

There are dozens of books offering variations on the standard interpretations as well as several which offer the authors' own idiosyncratic versions. We believe that as far as traditional interpretations go Eden Gray still leads the pack for simplicity and clarity. Hers is certainly the best conventional book to *start* with.

Bill Butler, *Dictionary of the Tarot*, Schocken (New York), 1975.

Butler's book summarizes card by card, including the minor arcana, the interpretations given by the major conventional commentators.

Paul Foster Case, *The Tarot*, Macoy (Richmond, Virginia), 1947.

Case was a member of the Golden Dawn, and formed his own (not secret) society, the Brotherhood of the Adytum. This group, located in Los Angeles, was (and is) heavily involved with the Tarot. Case's BOTA deck is quite similar to Waite-Smith's—which is not surprising since both are offspring of the Golden Dawn deck. Case's book focuses on the complex meanings of the major arcana.

Aleister Crowley, *The Book of Thoth*, Samuel Weiser (New York), 1971.

Also a member of the Golden Dawn—from which he was expelled for unethical behavior—Crowley's book emphasizes the Egyptian and Kabbalistic origins of the Tarot. His interpretations, although distinctively his own, are heavily influenced by the Golden Dawn. Crowley's book is important for anyone seriously interested in the Tarot—but be cautious: this man had a strange history and was an inveterate woman-hater.

Eden Gray, *A Complete Guide to the Tarot*, Bantam (New York), 1972.

It is a comprehensive *beginning* guide.

Jewels of the Wise, Epiphany Press (San Francisco), 1979.

If you can ignore the Christian coloring, this anonymously authored book on the Tarot and the Tree of Life can provide you with provocative insights into the meanings of the major arcana.

Rachel Pollack, *Seventy-Eight Degrees of Wisdom: A Book of the Tarot*, (Part I: The Major Arcana), The Aquarian Press (Wellingborough, England), 1980.

A very sensitive analysis of the meanings and contemporary psychological applications of the Tarot trumps.

Billie Potts, *A New Woman's Tarot*, Elf and Dragons Press (P.O. Box 609, Woodstock, N.Y. 12498), 1978.

This is the only publication we know of that has attempted a radical redesign of the Tarot from a Goddess-centered perspective. The cards are esthetically disappointing, but the content (the designations and interpretations) are well-researched and imaginative—if you want to move away from the historical Tarot. The interpretations include astrological and herbal correlations. Potts provides an interesting variation of the Celtic spread.

A.E. Waite, *A Pictorial Key to the Tarot*, Steiner Books (Blauvelt, New York), 1971.

Waite's book is divided into three parts: his version of the origins (somewhat obscured because of his Golden Dawn vows), his interpretations of the cards, and a section on spreads and divination.

Robert Wang, *An Introduction to the Golden Dawn Tarot*, Weiser (New York), 1978.

This book purports to give the "true" and unveiled explanation of the Golden Dawn Tarot system. It is a companion piece to the deck of cards, recently published, painted by Wang. This new "Golden Dawn" deck is supposed to be directly derived from an original Golden Dawn deck in the possession of Israel Regardie, an eminent occultist who was Crowley's secretary for several years. The new deck is far from appealing. Whether that is Wang's fault or not we don't know. But why wasn't the original deck simply published in its original form?

Jan Woudhuysen, *Tarot Therapy*, Tarcher (Los Angeles), 1980.

We dislike the cutsie drawings of the cards, and we totally disagree with the interpretations, but this book has genuine value in its thorough and down-to-earth sections on spreads and techniques of reading.

The Tarot and the Kabbalah:

Serious students of the Tarot sooner or later seem to be drawn to the Tree of Life, both as a spiritual system and as a vehicle for profound divination. This is a very difficult area of the Tarot, in which it takes real dedication and commitment to become adept. But it is well worth the effort. There are no easy starting books, no royal road to comprehension But for those who are interested, we would suggest the following:

Dion Fortune, *The Mystical Qabalah*, Ernest Benn (London), 1974.

Fortune is another member of the Golden Dawn and a well-known British psychoanalyst (Fortune is her *nom de plume*). Her book on the Kabbalah and Tarot, although difficult, is a good starting point.

Gareth Knight, *A Practical Guide to Qabalistic Symbolism*, 2 Vols., Weister (New York), 1965.

This work expands on Fortune's introduction. Volume One focuses on the Kabbalah; Volume Two deals with the paths on the Tree of Life. Perhaps the most important published work on this subject.

Gershom Scholem, *On the Kabbalah and Its Symbolism*, Schocken (New York), 1965.

The great Jewish scholar provides an indispensable background to understanding the history and meaning of the Kabbalah. (We recommend reading Wippler first, if you want an easier entry into the subject.)

Migene Wippler, *A Kabbalah for the Modern World*, Julian Press (New York), 1974.

A straightforward, modern elucidation of the teachings of the Kabbalah for the reader who wants to start with the ABC's of this complex subject. This is probably the best starting point.

Other books of interest from
ALYSON PUBLICATIONS

THE WANDERGROUND, by Sally Miller Gearhart, $9.00. Gearhart's stories imaginatively portray a future women's culture, combining a control of mind and matter with with a sensuous adherence to their own realities.

BUSHFIRE, edited by Karen Barber, $9.00. Amidst our differences, all lesbians share one thing: a desire for women. Sometimes intensely sexual, other times subtly romantic, this emotion is always incredibly powerful. These short stories celebrate lesbian desire in all its forms.

CHOICES, by Nancy Toder, $9.00. In this straightforward, sensitive novel, Nancy Toder conveys the joys — and fears — of a woman coming to terms with her attraction to other women.

BETWEEN FRIENDS, by Gillian E. Hanscombe, $8.00. The four women in this book represent different outlooks, yet are tied together by the bonds of friendship. Through their experiences, Hanscombe shows the close relationship between politics and everyday lives.

UNBROKEN TIES, by Carol S. Becker, $10.00. Through a series of personal accounts and interviews, Dr. Carol Becker, a practicing psychotherapist, charts the various stages of lesbian breakups and examines the ways women maintain relationships with their ex-lovers.

SUPPORT YOUR LOCAL BOOKSTORE

Most of the books described here are available at your nearest gay or feminist bookstore, and many of them will be available at other bookstores. If you can't get these books locally, order by mail using this form.

Enclosed is $_____ for the following books. (Add $1.00 postage if ordering just one book. If you order two or more, we'll pay the postage.)

1._____

2._____

3._____

name:_____

address:_____

city:_____state:_____zip:_____

ALYSON PUBLICATIONS
Dept. J-52, 40 Plympton St., Boston, MA 02118

After December 31, 1994, please write for current catalog.